Tampa Bay Rays 2019

A Baseball Companion

Edited by Patrick Dubuque, Aaron Gleeman and Bret Sayre

Baseball Prospectus

Craig Brown and Dave Pease, Consultant Editors
Rob McQuown and Harry Pavlidis, Statistics Editors

Copyright © 2019 by DIY Baseball, LLC.
All rights reserved

This book or any part thereof may not be reproduced or transmitted in any form or by any means, electronic or mechanical, including photocopying, recording, or by any information storage and retrieval system, without permission in writing from the publisher.

Limit of Liability/Disclaimer of Warranty: While the publisher and the author have used their best efforts in preparing this book, they make no representations or warranties with respect to the accuracy or completeness of the contents of this book and specifically disclaim any implied warranties of merchantability or fitness for a particular purpose. No warranty may be created or extended by sales representatives or written sales materials. The advice and strategies contained herein may not be suitable for your situation. You should consult with a professional where appropriate. Neither the publisher nor the author shall be liable for any loss of profit or any other commercial damages, including but not limited to special, incidental, consequential, or other damages.

Library of Congress Cataloging-in-Publication Data:
paperback
ISBN-13: 978-1-949332-24-7

Project Credits
Cover Design: Kathleen Dyson
Interior Design and Production: Jeff Pease, Dave Pease
Layout: Jeff Pease, Dave Pease

Baseball icon courtesy of Uberux, from https://www.shareicon.net/author/uberux

Ballpark diagram courtesy of Lou Spirito/THIRTY81 Project, https://thirty81project.com/

Manufactured in the United States of America
10 9 8 7 6 5 4 3 2 1

Table of Contents

Foreword v
    Rob Mains

Statistical Introduction vii

Part 1: Team Analysis

Table for Two: Previewing the 2019 Tampa Bay Rays 3
    Zach Crizer and Brian Duricy

Performance Graphs 7

2018 Team Performance 8

2019 Team Projections 9

Team Personnel 10

Tropicana Field Stats 11

Rays Team Analysis 13

Part 2: Player Analysis

Rays Player Analysis 22

Rays Prospects 99

Part 3: Featured Articles

The Hole in The Shift is Fixing Itself 115
    Russell Carleton

The State of the Quality Start 119
    Rob Mains

Heads-Up Hacking—The First Pitch 125
    Matthew Trueblood

A Hymn for the Index Stat 131
    Patrick Dubuque

Index of Names 135

Foreword

Rob Mains

Welcome to this companion of the 2019 Tampa Bay Rays. We at Baseball Prospectus are excited to provide this analysis of the Rays.

Our website, Baseball Prospectus, is a leader in delivering high-quality commentary and data to baseball fans everywhere. To some, those words—commentary and data—appear mutually exclusive. There are people out there who believe that traditional analysis and advanced analytics must run on different paths. But the simplistic narrative of stats vs. traditionalists just isn't true. Every team's analytics department interacts with scouting, development, and major league operations with a common goal: Delivering a championship. New technologies, like radar tracking of pitch speeds and movement, enable talent evaluators to focus on qualitative aspects of pitching like mechanics and pitch sequencing. In-game strategies like infield shifts, based on batters' hit tendencies, help turn balls in play into outs. Hitters use information to adjust their swings to maximize run production.

All these numbers can seem, at best, intimidating, and at worst, counterproductive to the casual fan. Even as technology and analysis have embedded themselves deeply into the way teams run, it can often feel like statistics create a displacement between the viewer and the sport, breaking them out of the action. And yet every fan incorporates the numbers to some degree; stats like batting average and earned run average, so fundamental to how we talk about performance, are actually complicated formulas. They don't bother people because those formulas have become second nature, as easy to translate as the action on the field.

Along the way, new statistics have entered baseball's lexicon. You'll see some of them, like on-base percentage (which measures a batter's ability to get on base via walk, hit batter, or hit), OPS (on-base plus slugging), and average exit velocity (the speed of balls off a hitter's bat) on broadcasts. Others, like DRC+, might well be new to you. Some of them have been well-defined to the public, others haven't. That lack of context has created ambiguity. Fans know that a ball hit 100 mph is scorched, but does that mean extra bases? (Not if it's hit on the ground or high in the air it doesn't.)

For those who are amenable to them, the new statistics can increase the enjoyment and understanding of the game. They can help fans identify when a pitcher is tiring, when a stolen base or a bunt attempt makes sense (and, more often, when it doesn't), or how a team's lineup might be constructed. Websites like Baseball Prospectus add to that understanding by weaving metrics into the narrative of the game. That's the goal of this publication: to take some of the newer, more complicated statistics and make them as intuitive as the ones on the back of old baseball cards.

But you don't need to love analytics to love baseball. The fans at BP who worked together to write this guide are captivated first and foremost by the game itself. We're drawn to Aaron Judge's power, Francisco Lindor's glove, Billy Hamilton's speed and Patrick Corbin's slider and don't need numbers to tell us why they're so mesmerizing. The underlying statistics provide depth to the game that we all love.

We hope you'll find that this guide helps you better understand the Rays. Our analysts have studied the team's major league personnel and its minor league affiliates to identify their strengths and weaknesses, both the obvious ones and those that only a careful dissection of players' performances—yes, including the data—can reveal. You don't need us to tell you who was good and who wasn't in 2018, but our models and writers can help you project how each player is going to perform this year and beyond, and appreciate the greatness of each new game as it unfolds. As in the sport itself, the human and analytic components combine to generate a deeper overall understanding.

Think back to the first time you saw a baseball game on a high-definition TV. You'd grown familiar with how the game looked and felt on a picture tube. But new TV allowed you to see details that you'd never seen before. That's how advanced statistics work. The game itself is why you're here and why you're buying this. (And, for that matter, why we wrote it.) The statistical measures provide the sharper focus, the detail, the depth of knowledge that you didn't have before, generating an overall superior picture. Enjoy the view.

—*Rob Mains is an author of Baseball Prospectus.*

Statistical Introduction

Sports are, fundamentally, a blend of athletic endeavor and storytelling. Baseball, like any other sport, tells its stories in so many ways: in the arc of a game from the stands or a season from the box scores, in photos, or even in numbers. At Baseball Prospectus, we understand that statistics don't replace observation or any of baseball's stories, but complement everything else that makes the game so much fun.

What stats help us with is with patterns and precision, variance and value. This book can help you learn things you may not see from watching a game or hundred, whether it's the path of a career over time or the breadth of the entire MLB. We'd also never ask you to choose between our numbers and the experience of viewing a game from the cheap seats or the comfort of your home; our publication combines running the numbers with observations and wisdom from some of the brightest minds we can find. But if you *do* want to learn more about the numbers beyond what's on the backs of player jerseys, let us help explain.

Offense

At the end of this past year, we've revised our methodology for determining batting value. Long-time readers of Baseball Prospectus will notice that we've retired True Average in favor of a new metric: Deserved Runs Created Plus (DRC+). Developed by Jonathan Judge and our stats team, this statistic measures everything a player does at the plate–reaching base, hitting for power, making outs, and moving runners over–and puts it on a scale where 100 equals league-average performance. A DRC+ of 150 is terrific, a DRC+ of 100 is average, and a DRC+ of 75 means you better be an excellent defender.

DRC+ also does a better job than any of our previous metrics in taking contextual factors into account. The model adjusts for how the park affects performance, but also for things like the talent of the opposing pitcher, value of different types of batted-ball events, league, temperature, and other factors. It's able to describe a player's expected offensive contribution than any other statistic we've found over the years, and also does a better job of predicting future performance as well.

The other aspect of run-scoring is baserunning, which we quantify using Baserunning Runs. BRR not only records the value of stolen bases (or getting caught in the act), but also accounts for a runner's ability to go first to third on a single or advance on a fly ball.

Defense

Where offensive value is *relatively* easy to identify and understand, defensive value is … not. Over the past dozen years, the sabermetric community has focused mostly on stats based on zone data: a real-live human person records the type of batted ball and estimated landing location, and models are created that give expected outs. From there, you can compare fielders' actual outs to those expected ones. Simple, right?

Unfortunately, zone data has two major issues. First, zone data is recorded by commercial data providers who keep the raw data private unless you pay for it. (All the statistics we build in this book and on our website use public data as inputs.) That hurts our ability to test assumptions or duplicate results. Second, over the years it has become apparent that there's quite a bit of "noise" in zone-based fielding analysis. Sometimes the conclusions drawn from zone data don't hold up to scrutiny, and sometimes the different data provided by different providers don't look anything alike, giving wildly different results. Sometimes the hard-working professional stringers or scorers might unknowingly inflict unconscious bias into the mix: for example good fielders will often be credited with more expected outs despite the data, and ballparks with high press boxes tend to score more line drives than ones with a lower press box.

Enter our Fielding Runs Above Average (FRAA). For most positions, FRAA is built from play-by-play data, which allows us to avoid the subjectivity found in many other fielding metrics. The idea is this: count how many fielding plays are made by a given player and compare that to expected plays for an average fielder at their position (based on pitcher ground-ball tendencies and batter handedness). Then we adjust for park and base-out situations.

When it comes to catchers, our methodology is a little different thanks to the laundry list of responsibilities they're tasked with beyond just, well, catching and throwing the ball. By now you've probably heard about "framing" or the art of making umpires more likely to call balls outside the strike zone for strikes. To put this into one tidy number, we incorporate pitch tracking data (for the years it exists) and adjust for important factors like pitcher, umpire, batter, and home-field advantage using a mixed-model approach. This grants us a number for how many strikes the catcher is personally adding to (or subtracting from) his pitchers' performance … which we then convert to runs added or lost using linear weights.

Framing is one of the biggest parts of determining catcher value, but we also take into account blocking balls from going past, whether a scorer deems it a passed ball or a wild pitch. We use a similar approach–one that really benefits from the pitch tracking data that tells us what ends up in the dirt and what doesn't. We also include a catcher's ability to prevent stolen bases and how well they field balls in play, and *finally* we come up with our FRAA for catchers.

Pitching

Both pitching and fielding make up the half of baseball that isn't run scoring: run prevention. Separating pitching from fielding is a tough task, and most recent pitching analysis has branched off from Voros McCracken's famous (and controversial) statement, "There is little if any difference among major-league pitchers in their ability to prevent hits on balls hit in the field of play." The research of the analytic community has validated this to some extent, and there are a host of "defense-independent" pitching measures that have been developed to try and extricate the effect of the defense behind a hurler from the pitcher's work.

Our solution to this quandary is Deserved Run Average (DRA), our core pitching metric. DRA looks like earned run average (ERA), the tried-and-true pitching stat you've seen on every baseball broadcast or box score from the past century, but it's very different. To start, DRA takes an event-by-event look at what the pitchers does, and adjusts the value of that event based on different environmental factors like park, batter, catcher, umpire, base-out situation, run differential, inning, defense, home field advantage, pitcher role, and temperature. That mixed model gives us a pitcher's expected contribution, similar to what we do for our DRC+ model for hitters and FRAA model for catchers. (Oh, and we also consider the pitcher's effect on basestealing and on balls getting past the catcher.)

It's important to note that DRA is set to the scale of runs allowed per nine innings (RA9) instead of ERA, which makes DRA's scale slightly higher than ERA's. The reason for this is because ERA tends to overrate three types of pitchers:

1. Pitchers who play in parks where scorers hand out more errors. Official scorers differ significantly in the frequency at which they assign errors to fielders.
2. Ground-ball pitchers, because a substantial proportion of errors occur on grounders.
3. Pitchers who aren't very good. Better pitchers often allow fewer unearned runs than bad pitchers, because good pitchers tend to find ways to get out of jams.

Since the last time you picked up an edition of this book, we've also made a few minor changes to DRA to make it better. Recent research into "tunneling"–the act of throwing consecutive pitches that appear similar from a batter's point of view until after the swing decision point–data has given us a new contextual factor to account for in DRA: plate distance. This refers to the distance between successive pitches as they approach the plate, and while it has a smaller effect than factors like velocity or whiff rate, it still can help explain pitcher strikeout rate in our model.

New Pitching Metrics for 2019

We're including a few "new" pitching metrics for 2019's suite of Baseball Prospectus publications, but you may be familiar with them if you've spent time scouring the internet for stats.

Fastball Percentage

Our fastball percentage (FB%) statistic measures how frequently a pitcher throws a pitch classified as a "fastball," measured as a percentage of overall pitches thrown. We qualify three types of fastballs:

1. The traditional four-seam fastball;
2. The two-seam fastball or sinker;
3. "Hard cutters," which are pitches that have the movement profile of a cut fastball and are used as the pitcher's primary offering or in place of a more traditional fastball.

For example, a pitcher with a FB% of 67 throws any combination of these three pitches about two-thirds of the time.

Whiff Rate

Everybody loves a swing and a miss, and whiff rate (WHF) measures how frequently pitchers induce a swinging strike. To calculate WHF, we add up all the pitches thrown that ended with a swinging strike, then divide that number by a pitcher's total pitches thrown. Most often, high whiff rates correlate with high strikeout rates (and overall effective pitcher performance).

Called Strike Probability

Called Strike Probability (CSP) is a number that represents the likelihood that all of a pitcher's pitches will be called a strike while controlling for location, pitcher and batter handedness, umpire and count. Here's how it works: on each pitch, our model determines how many times (out of 100) that a similar pitch was called for a strike given those factors mentioned above, and when normalized for each batter's strike zone. Then we average the CSP for all pitches thrown by a pitcher in a season, and that gives us the yearly CSP percentage you see in the stats boxes.

As you might imagine, pitchers with a higher CSP are more likely to work in the zone, where pitchers with a lower CSP are likely locating their pitches outside the normal strike zone, for better or for worse.

Projections

Many of you aren't turning to this book just for a look at what a player has done, but for a look at what a player is going to do: the PECOTA projections. PECOTA, initially developed by Nate Silver (who has moved on to greater fame as a political analyst), consists of three parts:

1. Major-league equivalencies, which use minor-league statistics to project how a player will perform in the major leagues;
2. Baseline forecasts, which use weighted averages and regression to the mean to estimate a player's current true talent level; and
3. Aging curves, which uses the career paths of comparable players to estimate how a player's statistics are likely to change over time.

With all those important things covered, let's take a look at what's in the book this year.

Team Prospectus

You bought this book to learn more about your favorite (or maybe least-favorite, who are we to judge?) team, so let's talk about them. After a thoughtful preview of the 2019 season, you'll be presented with our Team Prospectus. This outlines many of the key statistics for each team's 2018 season, as well as a very inviting stadium diagram.

First you'll find the Performance Graphs page. The first is the 2018 Hit List Ranking. This shows our Hit List Rank for the team on each day of the 2018 season and is intended to give you a picture of the ups and downs of the team's season, including their highest and lowest ranks of the year. Hit List Rank measures overall team performance and drives the Hit List Power Rankings at the baseballprospectus.com website.

The second graph is Committed Payroll and helps you see how the team's payroll has compared to the MLB and divisional average payrolls over time. Payroll figures are currents as of January 1, 2019; with so many free agents still unsigned as of this writing, the final 2018 figure will likely be significantly different for many teams. (In the meantime, you can always find the most current data at Baseball Prospectus' Cot's Baseball Contracts page.)

The third graph is Farm System Ranking and displays how the Baseball Prospectus prospect team has ranked the organization's farm system since 2007. It also indicates the highest and lowest ranks that the farm system achieved over that time.

We start the Team Performance page with the squad's unadjusted and third-order 2018 win-loss records, presented in divisional context. We then list the three highest performing hitters and pitchers by WARP for 2018. Beneath that are a host of other team statistics. **Pythag** presents an adjusted 2018 winning percentage, calculated by taking runs scored per game (**RS/G**) and runs allowed per game (**RA/G**) for the team, and running them through a version of Bill James' Pythagorean formula that was refined and improved by David Smyth and Brandon Heipp. (The formula is called "Pythagenpat," which is equally fun to type and to say.)

Next up is **DRC+**, described earlier, to indicate the overall hitting ability of the team either above or below league-average. Run prevention on the pitching side is covered by **DRA** (also mentioned earlier) and another metric: Fielding Independent Pitching (**FIP**), which calculates another ERA-like statistic based on strikeouts, walks, and home runs recorded. Defensive Efficiency Rating (**DER**) tells us the percentage of balls in play turned into outs for the team, and is a quick fielding shorthand that rounds out run prevention.

After that, we have several measures related to roster composition, as opposed to on-field performance. **B-Age** and **P-Age** tell us the average age of a team's batters and pitchers, respectively. **Salary** is the combined team payroll for all on-field players, and Doug Pappas' Marginal Dollars per Marginal Win (**M$/MW**) tells us how much money a team spent to earn production above replacement level.

Ending this batch of statistics is the number of disabled list days a team had over the season (**DL Days**) and the amount of salary paid to players on the disabled list (**$ on DL**); this final number is expressed as a percentage of total payroll.

Next to each of these stats, we've listed each team's MLB rank in that category from 1st to 30th. In this, 1st always indicates a positive outcome and 30th a negative outcome, except in the case of salary–1st is highest.

The Team Projections page is intended to convey the team's operational capacity entering the 2019 season. We start with the team's PECOTA projected record for 2019, again in divisional context. The **+/-** column indicates how many more or less wins the team is projected to get than they got in 2018. We then list the three highest projected hitters and pitchers by WARP for 2018. A brief farm system summary follows, with the team's top prospect and number of BP Top 101 Prospects. Finally, we list the key new players and departed players, along with their 2019 projected WARP.

Alex Bregman 3B

Born: 03/30/94 Age: 25 Bats: R Throws: R
Height: 6'0" Weight: 180 Origin: Round 1, 2015 Draft (#2 overall)

YEAR	TEAM	LVL	AGE	PA	R	2B	3B	HR	RBI	BB	K	SB	CS	AVG/OBP/SLG
2016	CCH	AA	22	285	54	16	2	14	46	42	26	5	3	.297/.415/.559
2016	FRE	AAA	22	83	17	6	0	6	15	5	12	2	1	.333/.373/.641
2016	HOU	MLB	22	217	31	13	3	8	34	15	52	2	0	.264/.313/.478
2017	HOU	MLB	23	626	88	39	5	19	71	55	97	17	5	.284/.352/.475
2018	HOU	MLB	24	705	105	51	1	31	103	96	85	10	4	.286/.394/.532
2019	HOU	MLB	25	675	96	38	3	23	78	73	107	12	4	.272/.359/.463

Breakout: 6% Improve: 52% Collapse: 5% Attrition: 2% MLB: 100%
Comparables: Anthony Rendon, David Wright, Pablo Sandoval

YEAR	TEAM	LVL	AGE	PA	DRC+	VORP	BABIP	BRR	FRAA	WARP
2016	CCH	AA	22	285	172	38.9	.286	1.6	SS(51): -3.4, 3B(11): 1.4	2.7
2016	FRE	AAA	22	83	161	10.0	.333	-1.2	SS(14): 2.1, LF(3): -0.1	0.8
2016	HOU	MLB	22	217	107	9.6	.317	0.5	3B(40): 0.9, SS(6): -0.1	1.1
2017	HOU	MLB	23	626	114	34.7	.311	-1.5	3B(132): 8.7, SS(30): -2.9	3.9
2018	HOU	MLB	24	705	150	72.6	.289	-1.6	3B(136): 5.4, SS(28): -0.4	7.4
2019	HOU	MLB	25	675	125	37.3	.295	0.0	3B 7, SS 0	4.6

After the projections page, we share a few items about the team's home ballpark. There's the aforementioned diagram of the park's dimensions (including distances to the outfield wall), a few important biographical facts about the stadium, a graphic showing the height of the wall from the left-field pole to the right-field pole, and a table showing three-year park factors for the stadium. The park factors are displayed as indexes where 100 is average, 110 means that the park inflates the statistic in question by 10 percent, and 90 means that the park deflates the statistic in question by 10 percent.

Following the ballpark page, we have a **Personnel** section that lists many of the important decision-makers and upper-level field and operations staff members for the franchise, as well as any former Baseball Prospectus staff members who are currently part of the organization.

Position Players

After all that information and a thoughtful bylined essay covering each team, we present our player comments. Each player is listed with the major-league team who employed him as of early January 2019. If a player changed teams after that point via free agency, trade, or any other method, you'll be able to find them in the book for their previous squad.

First, we cover biographical information (age is as of June 30, 2019) before moving onto the stats themselves. Our statistic columns include standard identifying information like **YEAR**, **TEAM**, **LVL** (level of affiliated play) and **AGE** before getting into the numbers. Next, we provide raw, unstranslated numbers like you might find on the back of your dad's baseball cards: **PA** (plate appearances), **R** (runs), **2B** (doubles), **3B** (triples), **HR** (home runs), **RBI** (runs batted in), **BB** (walks), **K** (strikeouts), **SB** (stolen bases) and **CS** (caught stealing). Then we have unadjusted "slash" statistics: **AVG** (batting average), **OBP** (on-base percentage) and **SLG** (slugging percentage).

Just below the stats box is **PECOTA** data, which is discussed further in a following section. After that, it's on to a pithy and always-informative comment written by a member of the Baseball Prospectus staff, before we cover more stats.

The second text box repeats YEAR, TEAM, LVL, AGE, and PA, then moves on to **DRC+** (Deserved Runs Created Plus), which we described earlier as total offensive expected contribution compared to the league average. Next, one of our oldest active metrics, **VORP** (Value Over Replacement Player), considers offensive production, position and plate appearances. In essence, it is the number of runs contributed beyond what a replacement-level player at the same position would contribute if given the same percentage of team plate appearances. VORP does not consider the quality of a player's defense.

BABIP (batting average on balls in play) tells us how often a ball in play fell for a hit, and can help us identify whether a batter may have been lucky or not ... but note that high BABIPs also tend to follow the great hitters of our time, as well as speedy singles hitters who put the ball on the ground.

The next item is **BRR** (Baserunning Runs), which covers all of a player's baserunning accomplishments which includes (but isn't limited to) swiped bags and failed attempts. Next is **FRAA** (Fielding Runs Above Average), which also includes the number of games previously played at each position noted in parentheses. Multi-position players have only their two most frequent positions listed here, but their total FRAA number reflects all positions played.

Our last column here is **WARP** (Wins Above Replacement Player). WARP estimates the total value of a player, which means for hitters it takes into account hitting runs above average (calculated using the DRC+ model), BRR and FRAA. Then, it makes an adjustment for positions played and gives the player a credit for plate appearances based upon the difference between "replacement level"¬–which is derived from the quality of players added to a team's roster after the start of the season¬–and the league average.

Catchers

Catchers are a special breed, and thus they have earned their own separate box which displays some of the defensive metrics that we've built just for them. As an example, let's check out J.T. Realmuto.

YEAR	TEAM	P. COUNT	FRM RUNS	BLK RUNS	THRW RUNS	TOT RUNS
2016	MIA	18935	-8.5	1.8	2.1	-5.6
2017	MIA	18959	5.3	1.7	1.0	9.1
2018	MIA	16399	-0.4	0.9	0.1	0.4
2019	PHI	18448	-1.4	1.5	0.7	0.8

The **YEAR** and **TEAM** columns match what you'd find in the other stat box. **P. COUNT** indicates the number of pitches thrown while the catcher was behind the plate, including swinging strikes, fouls, and balls in play. **FRM RUNS** is the total run value the catcher provided (or cost) his team by influencing the umpire to call strikes where other catchers did not. **BLK RUNS** expresses the total run value above or below average for the catcher's ability to prevent wild pitches and passed balls. **THRW RUNS** is calculated using a similar model as the previous two statistics, and it measures a catcher's ability to throw out basestealers but also to dissuade them from testing his arm in the first place. It takes into account factors like the pitcher (including his delivery and pickoff move) and baserunner (who could be as fast as Billy Hamilton or as slow as Yonder Alonso). **TOT RUNS** is the sum of all of the previous three statistics.

Pitchers

Let's give our pitchers a turn, using 2018 NL Cy Young winner Jacob deGrom as our example. Take a look at his first stat block: the first line and the **YEAR**, **TEAM**, **LVL** and **AGE** columns are the same as in the position player example earlier.

Here too, we have a series of columns that display raw, unadjusted statistics compiled by the pitcher over the course of a season: **W** (wins), **L** (losses), **SV** (saves), **G** (games pitched), **GS** (games started), **IP** (innings pitched), **H** (hits allowed) and **HR** (home runs allowed). Next we have two statistics that are rates: **BB/9** (walks per nine innings) and **K/9** (strikeouts per nine innings), before returning to the unadjusted **K** (strikeouts).

Next up is **GB%** (ground ball percentage), which is the percentage of all batted balls that were hit in the ground, including both outs and hits. Remember, this is based on observational data and subject to human error, so please approach this with a healthy dose of skepticism.

BABIP (batting average on balls in play) is calculated using the same methodology as it is for position players, but it often tells us more about a pitcher than it does a hitter. With pitchers, a high BABIP is often due to poor defense or bad luck, and can often be an indicator of potential rebound, and a low BABIP may be cause to expect performance regression. (A typical league-average BABIP is close to .290-.300.)

After a witty 150ish words on the player like only Baseball Prospectus's staff can provide, it's on to that second stat block, which repeats the YEAR, TEAM, LVL, and AGE columns. The metrics **WHIP** (walks plus hits per inning pitched) and **ERA** (earned run average) are old standbys: WHIP measures walks and hits allowed on a per-inning basis, while ERA measures earned runs on a nine-inning basis. Neither of these stats are translated or adjusted.

DRA (Deserved Run Average) was described at length earlier, and measures how many runs the pitcher "deserved" to allow per nine innings. Please note that since we lack all the data points that would make for a "real" DRA for minor-league events, the DRA displayed for minor league partial-seasons is based off of different data. (That data is a modified version of our cFIP metric, which you can find more information about on our website.)

Jacob deGrom   RHP
Born: 06/19/88   Age: 31   Bats: L   Throws: R
Height: 6'4"   Weight: 180   Origin: Round 9, 2010 Draft (#272 overall)

YEAR	TEAM	LVL	AGE	W	L	SV	G	GS	IP	H	HR	BB/9	K/9	K	GB%	BABIP
2016	NYN	MLB	28	7	8	0	24	24	148	142	15	2.2	8.7	143	47%	.312
2017	NYN	MLB	29	15	10	0	31	31	201[1]	180	28	2.6	10.7	239	48%	.305
2018	NYN	MLB	30	10	9	0	32	32	217	152	10	1.9	11.2	269	48%	.281
2019	NYN	MLB	31	13	9	0	31	31	186	145	18	2.3	10.7	221	46%	.286

Breakout: 8%   Improve: 29%   Collapse: 28%   Attrition: 6%   MLB: 85%
Comparables: Erik Bedard, A.J. Burnett, CC Sabathia

YEAR	TEAM	LVL	AGE	WHIP	ERA	DRA	WARP	MPH	FB%	WHF	CSP
2016	NYN	MLB	28	1.20	3.04	3.30	3.5	96.3	59.6	12.1	47.2
2017	NYN	MLB	29	1.19	3.53	3.02	5.7	97.2	55.5	14.5	49.5
2018	NYN	MLB	30	0.91	1.70	2.09	8.0	98.2	52.1	16.3	48.4
2019	NYN	MLB	31	1.02	2.91	3.23	3.9	96.6	54.5	14.8	48.2

Just like with hitters, **WARP** (Wins Above Replacement Player) is a total value metric that puts pitchers of all stripes on the same scale as position players. We use DRA as the primary input for our calculation of WARP. You might notice that relief pitchers (due to their limited innings) may have a lower WARP than you were expecting or than you might see in other WARP-like metrics. WARP does not take leverage into account, just the actions a pitcher performs and the expected value of those actions ... which ends up judging high-leverage relief pitchers differently than you might imagine given their prestige and market value.

MPH gives you the pitcher's 95th percentile velocity for the noted season, in order to give you an idea of what the *peak* fastball velocity a pitcher possesses. Since this comes from our pitch tracking data, it is not publicly available for minor-league pitchers.

Finally, we display the three new pitching metrics we described earlier. **FB%** (fastball percentage) gives you the percentage of fastballs thrown out of all pitches. **WhiffRt** (whiff rate) tells you the percentage of swinging strikes induced out of all pitches. **CS Prob** (called strike probability) expresses the likelihood of all pitches thrown to result in a called strike, after controlling for factors like handedness, umpire, pitch type, count, and location.

PECOTA

All players have PECOTA projections for 2019, as well as a set of other numbers that describe the performance of comparable players according to PECOTA. All projections for 2019 are for the player at the date we went to press in early January and are projected into the league and park context as indicated by the team abbreviation. All PECOTA projected statistics represent a player's projected major-league performance.

The numbers beneath the player's stats–Breakout, Improve, Collapse, Attrition–are part and parcel of the PECOTA projections. They estimate the likelihood of changes in performance relative to the player's previously-established level of production, based on the performance of comparable players:

Breakout Rate is the percent change that a player's production will improve by at least 20 percent relative to the weighted average of his performance over his most recent seasons.

Improve Rate is the percent chance that a player's production will improve at all relative to his baseline performance. A player who is expected to perform just the same as he has in the recent past will have an Improve Rate of 50 percent.

Collapse Rate is the percent chance that a position player's production will decline by at least 25 percent relative to his baseline performance.

Attrition Rate operates on playing time rather than performance. Specifically, it measures the likelihood that a player's playing time will decrease by at least 50 percent relative to his established level.

Breakout Rate and Collapse Rate can sometimes be counterintuitive for players who have already experienced a radical change in performance level. It's also worth noting that the projected decline in a player's rate performances might not be indicative of an expected decline in underlying ability or skill, but could just be an anticipated correction following a breakout season.

MLB% is the percentage of similar players who played in the major leagues in their relevant season.

The final pieces of information are the player's three highest-scoring comparable players as determined by PECOTA. All comparables represent a snapshot of how the listed player was performing at the same age as the current player, so if a 23-year-old pitcher is compared to Bartolo Colon, he's actually being compared to a 23-year-old Colon, not the version that pitched for the Rangers in 2018, nor to Colon's career as a whole.

A few points about pitcher projections. First, we aren't yet projecting peak velocity, so that column will be blank in the PECOTA lines. Second, projecting DRA is trickier than evaluating past performance, because it is unclear how deserving each pitcher will be of his anticipated outcomes. However, we know that another DRA-related statistic–contextual FIP or cFIP–estimates future run scoring very well. So for PECOTA, the projected DRA figures you see are based on the past cFIPs generated by the pitcher and comparable players over time, along with the other factors described above.

Lineouts

In each chapter's Lineouts section, you'll find abbreviated text comments, as well as most of same information you'd find in our full player comments. We limit the stats boxes in this section to only including the 2018 information for each player.

Exclusive Player Visualizations

In our constant battle to provide you with new and interesting baseball content you can't find anywhere else, we've added a trio of data visualizations to each hitter's entry in these books and a pair of visualizations for each pitcher.

For hitters, you'll find three new infographics. The first is each player's **Batted Ball Distribution**, which displays the five major sections of the field: LF (left), LCF (left center), CF (center), RCF (right center), and RF (right). The percentage indicated tells us what percentage of batted balls from that hitter fell within that part of the field during the 2018 season. We've also included the hitter's slugging percentage on balls in play (also called **SLGCON**) for that part of the field.

You'll also see two heatmaps: **Strike Zone vs LHP** and **Strike Zone vs RHP**. These heat maps represent a view of the strike zone from behind the catcher. Areas where there is a darker coloration represent the places where a higher percentage of pitches resulted in hits. In other words, the heatmap represents a hitter's "sweet spots" for getting hits against either left-handed or right-handed pitchers, depending on the image.

Pitchers get two images that help explain what their pitches look like from a hitter's perspective: **Pitch Shape vs LHH** and **Pitch Shape vs RHH**. These images show you the shape and the "tunneling" effect of each pitcher's offerings from the batter's perspective. For each type of pitch that a pitcher throws (represented by an indicator shape), there's a set of dots indicating the flight path, where each dot represents a 0.01-second interval. This maps the average trajectory and speed of an offering, ending where the ball crosses the plate. The solid black box represents the regular strike zone, while the gray contour lines indicate the range of locations that a pitcher typically works in.

Below the image, we provide a bit more detailed information about each pitcher's average offering in the **Pitch Types** box. Here, we also list each of the pitcher's major offerings under the **Type** column.

- **Fastballs** (which usually refers to the four-seam variation)
- **Sinkers** and/or two-seam fastballs
- **Cutters** (which could include "hard" cutters like cut fastballs and "soft" cutters that resemble hard sliders)
- **Changeups** (not including most splitters)
- **Splitters** (split-fingered pitches, forkballs, and some split-changes)
- **Sliders** and/or slurves
- **Curveballs** (including spike-curveballs and knuckle-curveballs, as well as some slurvy curves)
- **Slow curveballs** and/or eephus pitches
- **Knuckleballs**
- **Screwballs**

The **Freq** column indicates the percentage of overall pitches that fall into each of those type categories; if a pitcher has a 16.55% score for changeups, then that's the percent of all pitches that he throws as changeups. **Velo** is exactly what you think it is: the average miles per hour for each pitch type. **H Mov** is the number of inches of horizontal movement on the average pitch of that type, while **V Mov** is the number of inches of vertical movement on the average pitch of that type. (At Baseball Prospectus, we measure this over the long flight of the ball and include gravity into the V Mov number in order to give you the most realistic representation of what the pitch *actually* does.)

If you're wondering about the second number in brackets, that's the index for that velocity or movement compared to the league average. Like DRC+, a score of 100 means that the speed or movement is about the same as league average, while a higher score means that there's higher velocity or movement than the league average. Numbers below 100 indicate less velocity or movement than the league average.

Part 1: Team Analysis

Table for Two: Previewing the 2019 Tampa Bay Rays

Zach Crizer and Brian Duricy

How will this team end up, and what kind of path will they take to get there?

ZACH CRIZER: I wouldn't be surprised if they ended up in a similar position to the 2018 Rays. Predicting performance from a player, to a team, to a whole league—it gets murky fast. What we can see is that the Rays have a strong base of young talent, and many of them possess exceptional role or positional flexibility. In short, with openers, myriad Zobrist types and a two-way player being groomed in the minors, they look like a prototype for some next-generation baseball club.

There's little doubt they have the wherewithal to squeeze production out of what they have. What's less clear is how much juice is present in players like Joey Wendle, Daniel Robertson, Ryan Yarbrough and some of the bullpen arms. How many career years fueled last year's 90 wins?

Some new blood from a dynamite farm system, plus a few veteran reinforcements, will be worked in, but do you think that will provide enough of a counterweight to inevitable regression and push them toward October?

BRIAN DURICY: The effects from regression are likely to appear early—since 2009, they had six below-.500 March/April records—but that doesn't mean their October future will be decided in the first month. Of those six seasons, the Rays still finished with a first-half winning percentage above .500 four times. With that noted positional flexibility, and the fact that PECOTA projects only Willy Adames at shortstop to play a given position more than three-quarters of the time, the season's opening will be used to perfect their ideal scheme should they start slowly. And speaking of openings…

While the Rays may not be the only team deploying an opener regularly in 2019, pairing the strategy with the reigning AL Cy Young winner gives their pitching staff a unique quality. With Chris Archer gone and Jacob Faria taking a step backward with worse-than-average DRA- readings even in Triple-A last season, Blake Snell, Charlie Morton, and Tyler Glasnow should remain constants amongst a (no pun intended) rotating cast of minor league stars and opener veterans.

Their pitching will provide a strong baseline for contention, but with five of the projected starting position players sporting projected DRC+ numbers below 100 (and one exactly at 100), upper-decile performances at the plate are needed to keep up with the top of the AL East and hold off a handful of Wild Card hopefuls.

ZACH: With their trade acquisitions at last year's deadline striking a balance between right-now plays (Tommy Pham, Glasnow) and future focus (Shane Baz), it will be interesting to see how willing they are to push chips in for a 2019 run if they are indeed close to the Wild Card race. This is an organization that seems more likely to hoard prospects and hope their internal reinforcements do the trick. In this season's American League, that could be enough to play at least one game in October.

Who is the Rays' breakout player for 2019?

BRIAN: As you mentioned, last season saw a syncing of multiple breakout performances, so who do you see being 2019's Wendle (including, even, 2019 Wendle)?

ZACH: I'm not sure if I'd peg anyone as an actual Wendle parallel. Not many 28-year-old rookies put up 3-WARP seasons. A player who will be competing with Wendle for playing time might have a better outlook for 2019 and beyond. Brandon Lowe obliterated the upper minors last year and got his feet wet in the majors. His 105 DRC+ projection from PECOTA is the highest of any Tampa middle infielder, though he is likely to see time at first base, as well. With his pedigree and track record, he could seize a full-time role at the expense of Wendle, Robertson and company.

The other important bet the Rays are making is on Yandy Diaz—a musclebound, exit velo hero they acquired for Jake Bauers. He looks set for a healthy amount of plate appearances, but they'll need to solve the riddle of how to get him to hit the ball in the air. How do you like their chances of doing that? It's not as if Cleveland was ignoring this obvious, potentially impactful adjustment when Diaz was on their roster.

BRIAN: While Diaz hasn't altered his tendency to swing much across two limited major league seasons, he's already exhibited improvement in two key areas: reducing whiffs versus fastballs and dramatically increasing his contact rate outside the zone (by nearly 13 percentage points from 2017 to 2018). The results of that contact, however, may best be explained by the fact that across seven pitches, his GB/FB ratio is almost exclusively in the hundreds of percent, with a 3,800 percent mark for sinkers. So even though he hits the ball hard—and he absolutely does—some of that appeal is influenced by hitting grounders with power frequently. The Rays' belief that he can transfer that power to the air reflects the extra value they thrive on, but his potential to lead the team in OBP will provide benefits of its own.

As we watch for Diaz to fulfill his home run potential, Lowe may be playing a different position each time Diaz hits it out of the park. Lowe, while playing multiple positions, will still derive his greatest value from looking to recapture the elite DRC+ he showcased throughout the minors.

What part of the team can you simply not go along with PECOTA on?

ZACH: There are several eye-opening projections laid out for the Rays. They're tied with Yankees as the AL's third-best run prevention unit. Pham is projected as the club's best hitter. Their team slugging percentage leaves quite a bit to be desired—it begins with a three.

What would you push back on, were PECOTA a real, live human with a Twitter account (like many seem to think it is)?

BRIAN: Looking at their respective projection lines, one could be forgiven for confusing the upcoming seasons for Tyler Glasnow and Charlie Morton. The Rays should still see the value they're paying for in Morton, but DRA saw his journey to an upper-level starter as a more gradual one; Glasnow, on the other hand, had one disastrous season by DRA and two others of above-average pitching. His potential brings about a higher ceiling for 2019 than Morton, and I see PECOTA underselling Glasnow amidst a formidable top-three in the rotation.

ZACH: If they were to continue using Glasnow in his short burst roles, I think I'd agree that he'll likely perform better than PECOTA is giving him credit for. If he transitions into a more starter-like or bulk role, I don't think he has shown the command to limit homers and hard contact over six innings or more. The projected 11 homers across 130 innings of work squares with his minor league numbers (where his velocity was a rarer sight) but would be by far his best rate in the majors. I don't think he's going to hit that while simultaneously taking on more innings per outing.

The player PECOTA is undershooting in my eyes is Austin Meadows. He's always going to get the looming "when healthy" tag, but his bat has consistently shown up during his stretches of playing time. A 95 DRC+ in his 2018 debut involved some growing pains, but I don't see him plummeting to the 77 DRC+—with a total void where his OBP should be—that PECOTA projects. An average or better strikeout rate and some athleticism reads to me as a player likely to offer positive production.

On the less rosy side, the collective run prevention numbers PECOTA projects rely on some serious innings from promising but fresh-faced pitchers like Jalen Beeks and Diego Castillo. Beeks had a 5.51 ERA (and 5.46 DRA) in his major league sample, but projects at a 3.85 ERA over 70 innings. How much are you willing to buy another all-systems-go bullpen year?

BRIAN: I'm willing to buy that this is their strategy for the foreseeable future but I'm not entirely sold on the exact composition of that strategy. PECOTA's optimism may not be rewarded by Beeks this season, but that alone wouldn't spell the end of the bullpen-on-equal-footing mindset. Whereas he's projected for 70 innings, given the depth of the potential Opening Day bullpen staff plus some good arms still populating the upper minors, a poor start for somebody like Beeks would, in the immediate future, mean that those innings would shift to another pitcher. Colin Poche and Ian Gibaut, for instance, are projected for less than 50 innings combined. Both dominated Triple-A in 2018, and their 10+ K/9 lines should remain in the majors; the opportunity for additional innings, if available, will fall to them.

But if they, too, reflect even their 40th-percentile projections, then we're looking at your consideration of how willing Tampa Bay is to reverse course at the trade deadline and make a push for an impact free agent.

Overall, what do you predict the Rays' final record will be?

ZACH: Obviously, they're coming off a season that provides a lot of optimism for a leap into October this year, and that is very much on the table. However, their glut of young and/or out-of-nowhere hitters doesn't inspire confidence for me, and the pitching—even with some great pieces at the top and impressive bullpen arms—doesn't totally overwhelm my fears of regression. I'll peg them for 84 wins, a couple short of PECOTA, and another just-missed season.

BRIAN: PECOTA gives them the fifth and final spot of above-.500 teams in the American League, a five-game advantage over the Twins. The potential variance in just exactly which players exceed expectations means that five games, give or take, around their 86-win projection is a real possibility. I agree that they'll experience regression in some key areas, but with the lack of confidence PECOTA has in a Wild Card challenger, an 85-win, final Wild Card spot season will give them the playoff opportunity last year's 90 wins did not.

Performance Graphs

2018 Hit List Ranking

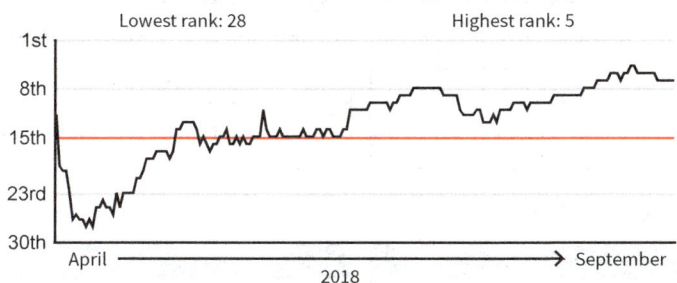

Committed Payroll (in millions)

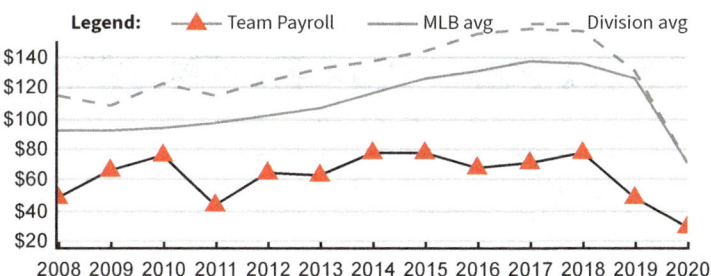

Farm System Ranking

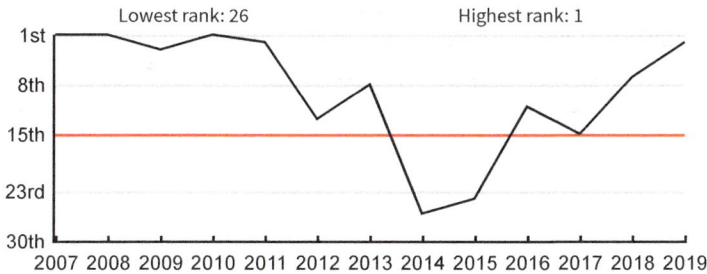

2018 Team Performance

ACTUAL STANDINGS

Team	W	L	Pct
BOS	108	54	.666
NYA	100	62	.617
TBA	**90**	**72**	**.555**
TOR	73	89	.450
BAL	47	115	.290

THIRD-ORDER STANDINGS

Team	W	L	Pct
NYA	99	63	.611
BOS	99	63	.611
TBA	**98**	**64**	**.604**
TOR	70	92	.432
BAL	54	108	.333

TOP HITTERS

Player	WARP
Joey Wendle	3.2
Matt Duffy	3.1
Daniel Robertson	2.1

TOP PITCHERS

Player	WARP
Blake Snell	6
Jose Alvarado	1.7
Sergio Romo	1.7

VITAL STATISTICS

Statistic Name	Value	Rank
Pythagenpat	.547	11th
Runs Scored per Game	4.42	16th
Runs Allowed per Game	3.99	5th
Deserved Runs Created Plus	98	13th
Deserved Run Average	4.01	8th
Fielding Independent Pitching	3.85	6th
Defensive Efficiency Rating	.722	2nd
Batter Age	27.1	5th
Pitcher Age	26.7	4th
Salary	$76.0M	28th
Marginal $ per Marginal Win	$1.5M	29th
Disabled List Days	$1,293.0M	21st
$ on DL	18%	17th

2019 Team Projections

PROJECTED STANDINGS

Team	W	L	Pct	+/-
NYA	96	66	.592	-4
BOS	90	72	.555	-18
TBA	**85**	**77**	**.524**	**-5**
TOR	76	86	.469	+3
BAL	57	105	.351	+10

TOP PROJECTED HITTERS

Player	WARP
Kevin Kiermaier	2.9
Tommy Pham	2.3
Mike Zunino	2.1

TOP PROJECTED PITCHERS

Player	WARP
Blake Snell	3.5
Charlie Morton	2.7
Tyler Glasnow	2.4

FARM SYSTEM REPORT

Top Prospect	Number of Top 101 Prospects
Wander Franco, #10	7

KEY DEDUCTIONS

Player	WARP
C.J. Cron	2.2
Carlos Gomez	1.3
Mallex Smith	1.0
Jake Bauers	0.3

KEY ADDITIONS

Player	WARP
Charlie Morton	2.7
Mike Zunino	2.1
Yandy Diaz	1.4
Avisail Garcia	1.0

Team Personnel

President of Baseball Operations
Matt Silverman

Senior Vice President
Chaim Bloom

SVP, General Manager
Erik Neander

Manager
Kevin Cash

BP Alumni
Chaim Bloom
James Click
Jason Cole

Tropicana Field Stats

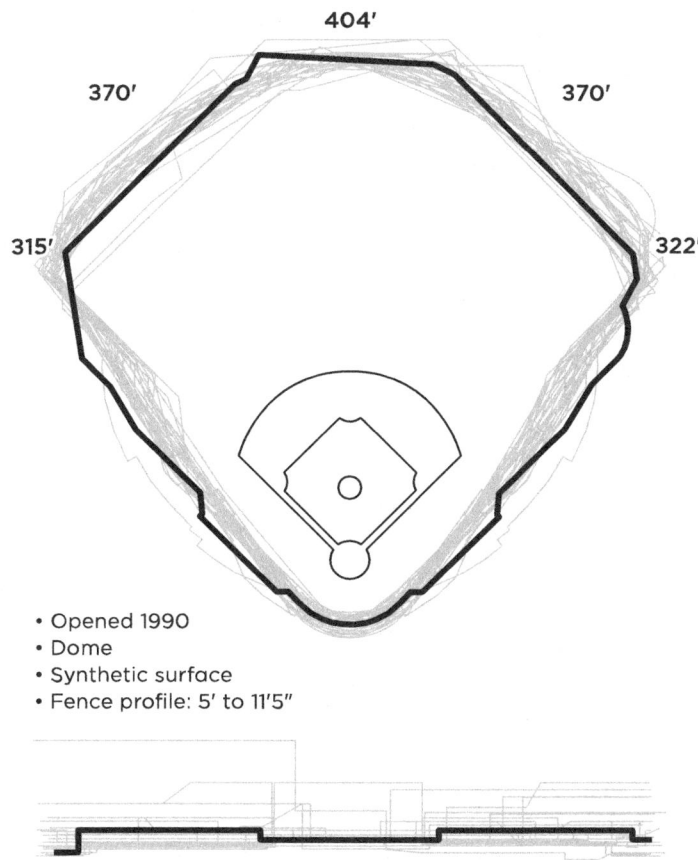

- Opened 1990
- Dome
- Synthetic surface
- Fence profile: 5′ to 11′5″

Three-Year Park Factors

Runs	Runs/RH	Runs/LH	HR/RH	HR/LH
95	95	95	96	95

Rays Team Analysis

On May 19, 2018, the Tampa Bay Rays did something relatively new: They began their game with relief ace Sergio Romo on the mound. In using Romo–a reliever through his career up until that day in May–for the first few batters of the game before going to another pitcher for the bulk of the innings, they implemented a role popularly called *"The Opener."* By regularly throwing a relief pitcher first–before going to the man who would normally be the starter–they threw players, fans, and (especially) the baseball media into a frenzy.

By the end of the season, the Rays had regularly implemented this strategy (though not as often as you might think) and surprised many by vaulting to a 90-72 record despite a bargain-basement payroll and a roster that never inspired the confidence that they would contend for a playoff appearance. With the opener strategy gaining traction with other organizations over the past year, it's probably important to answer two questions as best we can: (1) what exactly *is* an opener? and (2) did the strategy work for the Rays in 2018?

What is an opener? (Really?)

The Rays were not the first team in history to use a relief pitcher to start a baseball game before turning the ball over to a pitcher who would pitch the bulk of the remaining innings. However, they were the first team to try a long-term strategy like this, where a reliever would be tasked with getting the first out or three (or more, but no more than two innings) before passing the game on to a long-distance "starting" pitcher.

This strategy (and the term "opener") were popularized by a plucky young writer at *Beyond the Box Score* back in 2013[1] and can be defined using a couple of simple rules:

- The first pitcher in the game faces batters for no more than three innings.
- The second pitcher in the game faces batters for an intended term of no fewer than four innings.
- The strategy is used with some regularity over the course of a season.

(Before we go any further, I'd like to briefly address the issue of the second pitcher in an opener game, and what they should be called. If they don't begin the game, we can't call them a "starting pitcher," but the role is unique enough that it requires specific nomenclature. "Swingman" is more aligned with a different role–a pitcher who can be a traditional starter or a traditional relief pitcher–and the Rays' term "bulk guy" sounds vaguely derogatory or that all those pitchers should look like Bartolo Colon. So I'd like to recommend the term *yeoman* for pitchers who enter the game after the opener to pitch to the fifth or sixth inning and beyond.

You may know the term from the archaic role of woodsman or servant, or from the more recent military usage, but it fits for two reasons: the first is the adjectival use of the word, which implies loyally and valiantly completing a task that typically involves great labor. *Katrina did yeoman's work filing all of those Freedom of Information Act requests.* The second, lesser reason is that in older times, the yeoman was often an archer, and that seems to jive nicely with the pitching profession and emphasis on accuracy. I'll be using the term instead of "bulk guy" going forward.)

The opener strategy is not the same thing as two other reliever-based starting pitching strategies, both of which the Rays *also* tried in 2018. "Bullpenning" is when the team throws *only* relief pitchers over the course of a game, and differs from the opener in the lack of a yeoman role. It also is often a function of emergency when a team is without a scheduled starter and must improvise rather than a function of design. "Piggybacking" is when two pitchers throw a roughly-similar number of pitches or innings, and effectively split the lion's share of innings in a game equitably. Neither of these strategies are quite the same as the opener.

(Neither is a strategy that closely resembles the opener but without the same intention: when a team throws a starting pitcher who gets shelled early in the game and *must* be replaced to prevent further damage. I refer to this as the "Oriole-pener strategy.")

So why would a team try out this opener strategy, effectively casting aside over 100 years of starting pitcher tradition? In the years since my first article on the subject advocating for the role, I've identified a number of potential reasons why the strategy might be effective:

- An opener of opposing handedness than the yeoman may force a team to manage their platoons differently than usual early in the game, or restructure their lineup to a disadvantage
- An opener of significant skill may be able to limit run-scoring during the first inning, which is typically the highest run-scoring inning of any given game.

- An opener who is successful may give a team the psychic benefits that come from an early lead.
- An opener may face the more talented hitters at the top of the lineup, while allowing the yeoman to face the bottom of a lineup more frequently over the game.
- An opener role for a relief pitcher may give that pitcher a more comfortably-defined role, or allow them to be used more frequently due to scheduling.

On the other hand, there are noted cons to the opener strategy, which include:

- Using an opener forces a team to "burn" one of their relievers early, shortening the bullpen during high-leverage innings later in the game.
- Using an opener may make the yeoman have more trouble warming up or not have as defined of a pre-game schedule than if they were a regular starting pitcher.
- Using an opener that isn't successful (or a yeoman who must leave the game early) may tax a team's bullpen even more than a poor appearance would under normal circumstances.

In theory, the opener is a high-risk, high-reward strategy that's moderately aggressive…and therefore is theoretically a good fit for a team like the Rays, who would need a huge boost to surpass the high-talent, high-payroll Yankees and Red Sox. (The Rays' 90 wins in 2018 while using the occasional opener couldn't even crack the playoffs, for example.) But while the Rays had remarkable success last year, I'm not sure if we can effectively trace their win-loss record directly back to the use of openers. Let's see how far we can get.

Did the opener strategy work?

First, we've got to identify how many openers (and yeomen) were used by the Rays, when they were used, and who they were. In 2018, the Rays used 17 different starting pitchers, six of which could be considered openers using the criteria noted above. These standards resulted in 36 "opener games" thrown by the Rays in 2018. There were also a few dozen "bullpen" games and a small handful of "piggyback" games.

Opener	# of Opener Appearances
Ryne Stanek	16
Diego Castillo	6
Hunter Wood	6
Sergio Romo	4
Matt Andriese	1
Jonny Venters	1

The yeoman role for the Rays was only a bit more distributed, with seven different pitchers coming into games late as a "bulk guy." Stanek's counterpart–the yeoman among yeomen–was Ryan Yarbrough, who consistently filled the role throughout the season. Yarbrough was the team's first yeoman, serving in the role when Romo made the first opener start, and also filled in there into the last week of the season, supporting Diego Castillo's start on the 24th of September.

Yeoman	# of Yeoman Appearances
Ryan Yarbrough	15
Yonny Chirinos	9
Jalen Beeks	6
Austin Pruitt	3
Anthony Banda	1
Vidal Nuno	1
Ryan Weber	1

An interesting thing about the opener experiment is how much variation there was in pairings: it was a rarity for much of the season for the same opener and the same yeoman to match up consistently week after week. Ryan Yarbrough, by virtue of how many yeoman appearances he made over time, paired with all but one opener…only missing Matt Andriese's single start. But by August, a more formal pattern seemed to emerge: Ryne Stanek paired with Yonny Chirinos, and either Hunter Wood or Diego Castillo paired with Yarbrough.

When we start to try and identify whether or not the opener strategy worked, there's a bunch of challenges that face it. The strategy itself probably doesn't solely dictate whether or not the team wins a particular game: there are too many variables in play to attribute the win to one particular pitching strategy. Nevertheless, we should see whether or not the team won its 36 opener games. The Rays went 19-17 in games in which a true "opener" was used.

So if games won while using an opener aren't enough to tell us whether or not the strategy works, what could? My best theory on the matter is to look at projected pitcher performance for Tampa's pitchers used in the opener and yeoman roles, and compare that to their actual performance. Baseball Prospectus' PECOTA metric is an excellent tool for that comparison. With it, we can see how differently the pitchers themselves performed, perhaps in part due to their new roles.

Opener	PECOTA IP	Actual IP	PECOTA DRA	Actual DRA	PECOTA ERA	Actual ERA
Ryne Stanek	51	66.3	4.36	3.34	3.79	2.98
Diego Castillo	17	56.7	5.25	3.70	4.90	3.18
Hunter Wood	17	41	5.04	2.97	4.64	3.73
Sergio Romo	56.7	67.3	4.57	2.80	4.05	4.14
Matt Andriese	115	78.7	4.76	4.97	4.11	5.26
Jonny Venters	N/A	34.3	N/A	4.90	N/A	3.67

Yeoman	PECOTA IP	Actual IP	PECOTA DRA	Actual DRA	PECOTA ERA	Actual ERA
Ryan Yarbrough	45	147.3	5.26	4.82	4.56	3.91
Yonny Chirinos	37.7	89.7	4.94	4.23	4.43	3.51
Jalen Beeks	10.7	50.7	5.72	5.46	5.03	5.51
Austin Pruitt	90	69.7	5.05	3.66	4.37	4.65
Anthony Banda	50	14.7	5.10	4.75	4.42	3.68
Vidal Nuno	40	33	5.38	4.39	4.86	1.64
Ryan Weber	36.3	5.3	5.08	7.01	4.77	5.06

Certainly, I'm not trying to imply here that use in either an opener or a yeoman role correlated with or caused improved performance in any of the pitchers the Rays used in either role this year. But what we can see here is that very few of the pitchers the Rays used in either role suffered from it, when compared to what PECOTA projected for them this year. The players who saw the most action as either an opener or a yeoman (Yarbrough, Chirinos, Beeks, Pruitt, Stanek, Castillo, Wood, and Romo) all saw DRA numbers better than what was projected for them, and only three of them saw mild ERA rises from what was projected.

Comparing our openers' and yeomen's splits in games which they started or relieved hasn't provided much information, which is to be expected given how little data exists at this time. The pitchers who spent the most innings swapping between opener and "regular" reliever or yeoman and "starting" pitcher (like Stanek and Yarbrough) didn't show much difference between their DRA numbers as "starter" or "reliever."

These data points are certainly too few and too noisy to give us a certain answer as to whether or not the opener gambit was a success, consider this an answer to its efficacy: there are no signs that the opener gambit was a failure. The team won more games than it lost during opener appearances, the team's pitchers used in these roles were more effective than projected, and none of the team's pitchers used in these roles suffered significant injuries or voiced serious concerns about their use. If we can't insist that the use of openers was an unmitigated success on the field, perhaps we can at least rule out the fact that it caused the team to fail.

In part because we don't have certainty that the strategy was a success, more questions emerge than just the first two posed in this essay.

Were the Rays the right team to try the Opener?

Even before the season started, the Rays were a team without significant starting pitching. Chris Archer was a known quantity and something close to an ace, but top prospect Brent Honeywell suffered an injury, as did 2017 breakout starter Jacob Faria. Blake Snell was unproven, and not yet the 2018 Cy Young Award winner, and that left the team with few possible regular starting pitching options. While a lack of regular, reliable MLB-quality starting pitchers is a necessity to consider an opener strategy, the other side of it is having a deep, effective bullpen.

In this area, I'm not certain the Rays were a good fit for the strategy...and it makes me think that the opener strategy was more of a Plan B than their initial plan. Early in the year, with the Red Sox and Yankees looking unbeatable, the team shipped former closer Alex Colome to the Mariners as part of a deal that brought back cash savings and negligible prospect value. The Rays did not immediately reassign the payroll resources back to the big-league team, so one is left to assume that this was entirely a move to slough off costs, at the price of a well-regarded relief pitcher with experience in high-leverage situations.

Using an opener invariably means that a team is without depth at the end of their bullpen: in order to commit to using a reliever early, the team must sacrifice the possibility of using that player at the end of the game. Therefore, the team must be confident that their remaining relief options can be viable. This is why in all my previous documentation of the theory behind the opener, I've postulated that this is a strategy best served by teams with a strong and deep bullpen. The Rays absolutely did not fall into this category, as Colome might've been their best reliever at the time of his trade. Sergio Romo was probably the team's best relief pitcher at the time he was shifted into an opener role, which isn't ideal given how using an opener makes a team more vulnerable in high-leverage late-inning situations.

At the same time, the Rays used primarily right-handed pitchers in their opener and yeoman roles, with the exception of southpaw Ryan Yarbrough. A team that intended to use the opener to blow up opposing platoons might want a more diverse left-right balance in the bullpen than what the Rays demonstrated.

What will the Rays do in 2019?

Early word is that the Rays plan to use the opener again in 2019. After all, why wouldn't they? The team implemented the strategy in 2018, and won a considerable amount of games. At the same time, the few resources they've committed to the team at the time of this writing offer competing narratives. First, the Rays made yet *another* trade with the Mariners, this time to acquire a defensive specialist to play catcher: Mike Zunino. Zunino is a very well-regarded defender behind the plate with a particular talent for framing pitches. Adding him to the roster could significantly improve the team's run prevention, and provide a small-but-noticeable bump to the skills of each pitcher on the roster, thereby improving the team's overall quality of depth. If I were going to run an opener strategy, I would certainly focus on acquiring a good-framing catcher, even if it were at the expense of a talented young player like Mallex Smith.

The Rays also acquired a more traditional starting pitcher in Charlie Morton, who is coming off a pair of tremendous seasons for the Houston Astros. Morton, like Blake Snell, is unlikely to be part of any opener strategy. This doesn't preclude the Rays from using an opener frequently, but it does assign resources away from the bullpen and towards a different starting pitcher. Morton appears to provide a great deal more value than his free agent contract indicates, but the Rays probably still need to increase the talent level of both their openers and their yeomen, and Morton should be neither.

Should any team employ an opener?

There's a compelling argument to be made that the opener has ethical considerations that make it anti-player and pro-ownership. Teams that use an opener may be driving down arbitration costs for starting pitchers moved into a yeoman role or keeping talented relievers from accruing saves and holds. Since the arbitration process rewards most heavily performance in traditional roles and acquiring traditional statistical benchmarks, the strategy either intentionally or unintentionally could push down salaries for pre-arbitration players.

If any team really wanted to commit to openers as a regular part of their team strategy, they should probably be willing to sign openers and yeomen on the free agent market and pay them market rates before changing up their traditional roles. That would indicate that they believe in the strategy as what's best at winning baseball games, rather than what's best for keeping payrolls low. The Rays may believe the former, but judging from their long history of depressing player salaries, they may even more strongly desire the latter.

At any rate, success breeds imitation in baseball, and other teams are already at least experimenting with opener games of their own. My best guess is that some other team will employ openers in a more effective fashion in years to come, especially if they're willing to invest significant payroll in building an extraordinary collection of talent in the bullpen instead of the rotation. Whether good or bad for baseball or business, other teams will see the Rays' (perceived) success and try to build on it. But the Rays were the team who were desperate enough to try the strategy first, and will get to go down in history as the first team to really give it a shot. (Just don't give too much of the credit to Sergio Romo instead of Ryne Stanek, Ryan Yarbrough, and Yonny Chirinos.)

—*Bryan Grosnick is an author of Baseball Prospectus.*

1. Author, Plucky Young. Beyond the Box Score. "Replacing setup men with 'openers'". Accessed 28 December 2018. https://www.beyondtheboxscore.com/2013/11/26/5144934/openers-bullpen-usage-closers-setup-men-weird-baseball-all-the-luke-hochevar

Part 2: Player Analysis

Willy Adames SS

Born: 09/02/95   Age: 23   Bats: R   Throws: R
Height: 6'0"   Weight: 200   Origin: International Free Agent, 2015

YEAR	TEAM	LVL	AGE	PA	R	2B	3B	HR	RBI	BB	K	SB	CS	AVG/OBP/SLG
2016	MNT	AA	20	568	89	31	6	11	57	74	121	13	6	.274/.372/.430
2017	DUR	AAA	21	578	74	30	5	10	62	65	132	11	5	.277/.360/.415
2018	DUR	AAA	22	278	36	9	5	4	34	27	66	3	3	.286/.353/.412
2018	TBA	MLB	22	323	43	7	0	10	34	31	95	6	5	.278/.348/.406
2019	TBA	MLB	23	550	59	22	3	13	59	49	146	7	4	.245/.316/.381

Breakout: 14%   Improve: 44%   Collapse: 7%   Attrition: 16%   MLB: 76%
Comparables: Dansby Swanson, Marcus Semien, Eugenio Suarez

At some point in the next few years, Adames is going to piss off the baseball world in the best way possible: a bat flip, a celebration, saying something about unwritten rules, or hopefully all of the above. Adames is a swaggy middle infielder who took the reins at shortstop for good following the deadline trade of Adeiny Hechavarria. Adames, a smooth hitter with good contact skills and power, struggled in his first real shot at the big leagues, but was also hampered by sporadic usage and uncertainty about his role. Entrenched in the six spot, he hit .329/.406/.480 in 198 plate appearances from August 1 on. Adames introduced a shorter stroke during this return tour to the majors, which resulted in fewer strikeouts and more power. A .378 BABIP is something to watch for, but it's not like Adames was projected to be a glove-first player, although he has all the tools to stick at short even if his aggressive style leads to a few errors. He's a potential three-WARP player, with more upside left in the tank if everything breaks right.

YEAR	TEAM	LVL	AGE	PA	DRC+	VORP	BABIP	BRR	FRAA	WARP
2016	MNT	AA	20	568	131	47.0	.342	2.4	SS(112): 2.3	3.4
2017	DUR	AAA	21	578	121	35.8	.354	1.1	SS(117): 0.1, 2B(11): 0.5	3.1
2018	DUR	AAA	22	278	109	15.1	.367	1.5	SS(62): 2.4	1.5
2018	TBA	MLB	22	323	100	15.9	.378	2.3	SS(75): -6.7, 2B(10): 1.7	1.2
2019	TBA	MLB	23	550	94	21.0	.319	-0.6	SS 0	1.6

***Willy Adames**, continued*

Batted Ball Distribution

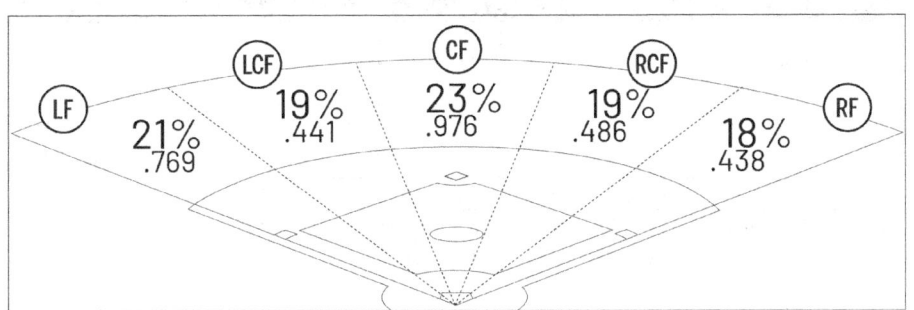

Strike Zone vs LHP   Strike Zone vs RHP

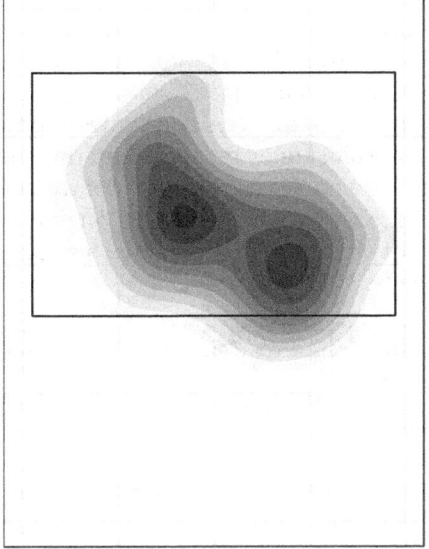

Christian Arroyo   INF
Born: 05/30/95   Age: 24   Bats: R   Throws: R
Height: 6'1"   Weight: 180   Origin: Round 1, 2013 Draft (#25 overall)

YEAR	TEAM	LVL	AGE	PA	R	2B	3B	HR	RBI	BB	K	SB	CS	AVG/OBP/SLG
2016	RIC	AA	21	517	57	36	1	3	49	29	72	1	1	.274/.316/.373
2017	SFN	MLB	22	135	9	5	0	3	14	8	32	1	2	.192/.244/.304
2017	SAC	AAA	22	102	18	7	0	4	16	6	12	2	0	.396/.461/.604
2018	TBA	MLB	23	59	5	2	1	1	6	6	16	0	0	.264/.339/.396
2018	DUR	AAA	23	182	19	12	0	2	20	8	32	2	3	.235/.286/.341
2019	TBA	MLB	24	58	6	3	0	1	6	3	13	0	0	.226/.281/.340

Breakout: 7%   Improve: 30%   Collapse: 1%   Attrition: 18%   MLB: 40%
Comparables: Giovanny Urshela, Willy Aybar, Daniel Murphy

The face of the franchise was altered forever when the Rays traded Evan Longoria to the Giants. As part of the return in that trade, it was a popular belief that Arroyo would replace Longoria at the hot corner before too long. Too long will have to be sometime in 2019, if not beyond. Arroyo did not have a great showing in 2018. He landed on the disabled list multiple times and played in just 68 combined games. He played 59 in 2017, giving him only 127 games since the end of 2016. He spent the bulk of his healthy time in Durham, where he hit .235 with an OPS under .650. Although it came in spurts, he was actually better in 20 games with the Rays and showed some of the bat and discipline traits that made him highly regarded entering the season. He has very good contact skills and is a multi-faceted defender who can play up the middle. The Rays have an immense amount of depth along the infield, so Arroyo is either going to have to start hitting again or diversify his portfolio. In either event, just being able to play is most important.

YEAR	TEAM	LVL	AGE	PA	DRC+	VORP	BABIP	BRR	FRAA	WARP
2016	RIC	AA	21	517	94	12.5	.313	-1.3	SS(48): -0.9, 3B(48): 2.1	0.8
2017	SFN	MLB	22	135	63	-6.3	.231	-2.8	3B(22): 1.4, SS(10): 0.9	0.0
2017	SAC	AAA	22	102	173	18.1	.427	0.5	SS(16): 0.6, 2B(5): -0.7	1.1
2018	TBA	MLB	23	59	86	3.6	.361	0.4	2B(8): -0.5, 3B(7): -0.5	0.0
2018	DUR	AAA	23	182	73	-0.3	.279	1.0	3B(34): -1.2, SS(6): -0.2	-0.2
2019	TBA	MLB	24	58	73	-0.3	.267	-0.1	3B 0, 2B 0	0.0

Christian Arroyo, continued

Batted Ball Distribution

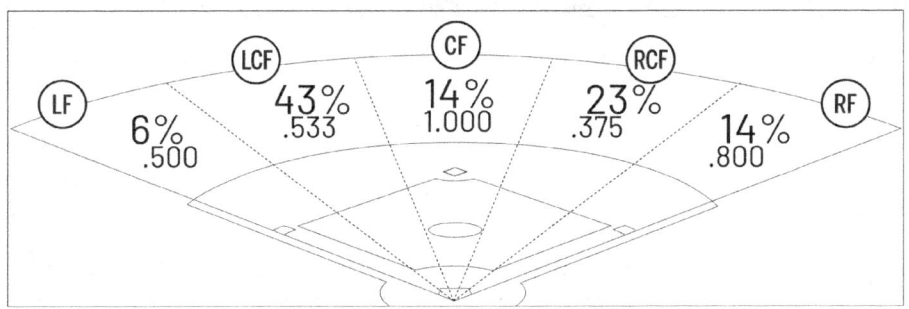

Strike Zone vs LHP   **Strike Zone vs RHP**

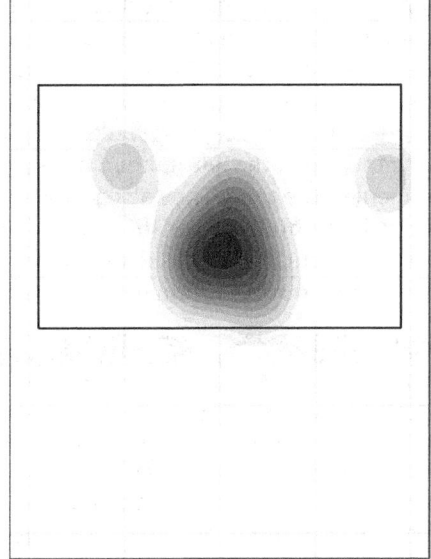

Ji-Man Choi   DH
Born: 05/19/91   Age: 28   Bats: L   Throws: R
Height: 6'1"   Weight: 230   Origin: International Free Agent, 2009

YEAR	TEAM	LVL	AGE	PA	R	2B	3B	HR	RBI	BB	K	SB	CS	AVG/OBP/SLG
2016	SLC	AAA	25	227	31	17	1	5	31	31	34	4	3	.346/.434/.527
2016	ANA	MLB	25	129	9	4	0	5	12	16	27	2	4	.170/.271/.339
2017	NYA	MLB	26	18	2	1	0	2	5	2	5	0	0	.267/.333/.733
2017	SWB	AAA	26	338	42	25	1	15	69	39	86	3	1	.288/.373/.538
2018	CSP	AAA	27	163	17	9	0	5	23	32	31	1	0	.302/.436/.488
2018	MIL	MLB	27	32	4	2	0	2	5	2	14	0	0	.233/.281/.500
2018	DUR	AAA	27	86	9	4	0	2	14	11	18	0	0	.270/.360/.405
2018	TBA	MLB	27	189	21	12	1	8	27	24	41	2	0	.269/.370/.506
2019	TBA	MLB	28	427	49	21	2	14	52	46	107	3	1	.238/.326/.417

Breakout: 6%   Improve: 30%   Collapse: 17%   Attrition: 28%   MLB: 71%
Comparables: Steve Pearce, Justin Bour, Nate Freiman

Chris Berman's favorite player (Gggggggg-man), Choi has always looked like he can hit the ball hard, but just recently started doing so. After being acquired from the Brewers in exchange for Brad Miller, the South Korea native smashed 25 extra-base hits in 221 plate appearances, including 10 that went back, back, back and gone. He showed a good approach at the plate, not chasing much out of the zone and accepting walks when they were given. The Rays were diligent in how they used the left-handed hitter, giving him the platoon advantage 89 percent of the time. They also gave him the advantage in the field, as in he played just three innings (first base) in 49 games with the team. For a team looking to cut fat from the margins, employing Choi as the strong side of a designated hitter platoon would accomplish that.

YEAR	TEAM	LVL	AGE	PA	DRC+	VORP	BABIP	BRR	FRAA	WARP
2016	SLC	AAA	25	227	151	12.8	.390	-4.7	1B(28): 1.6, LF(15): -0.9	0.8
2016	ANA	MLB	25	129	89	-3.6	.173	-0.1	1B(27): 2.2, LF(20): 0.1	0.3
2017	NYA	MLB	26	18	100	1.3	.222	-0.3	1B(6): 0.2	0.0
2017	SWB	AAA	26	338	138	22.7	.351	1.7	1B(57): 4.3	1.9
2018	CSP	AAA	27	163	144	12.3	.358	0.2	1B(38): -2.0, LF(1): 0.1	0.6
2018	MIL	MLB	27	32	103	0.6	.357	0.3	1B(2): 0.0, LF(1): 0.0	0.1
2018	DUR	AAA	27	86	120	2.9	.327	-0.9	1B(18): 0.2, LF(2): 0.0	0.1
2018	TBA	MLB	27	189	110	12.9	.310	1.9	1B(1): 0.0	0.7
2019	TBA	MLB	28	427	100	9.5	.293	-0.5	1B 1	0.9

Ji-Man Choi, continued

Batted Ball Distribution

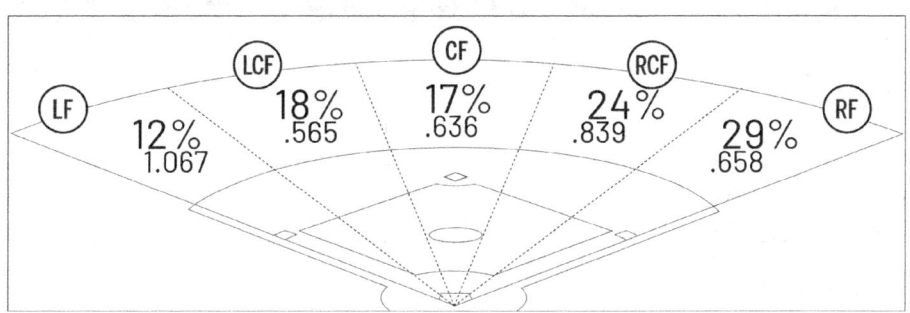

Strike Zone vs LHP   **Strike Zone vs RHP**

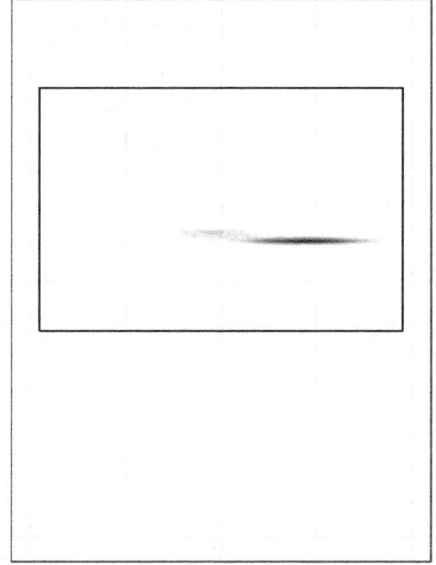 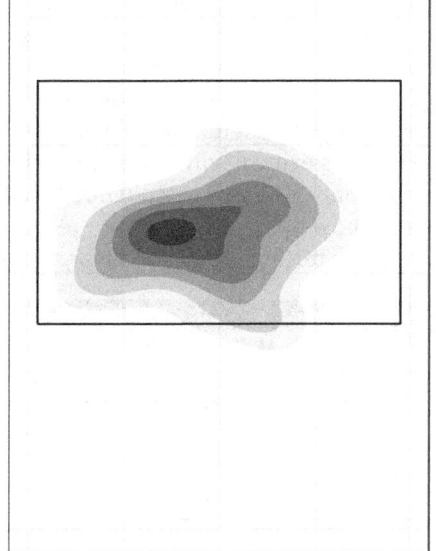

Yandy Diaz 3B

Born: 08/08/91 Age: 27 Bats: R Throws: R
Height: 6'2" Weight: 185 Origin: International Free Agent, 2013

YEAR	TEAM	LVL	AGE	PA	R	2B	3B	HR	RBI	BB	K	SB	CS	AVG/OBP/SLG
2016	AKR	AA	24	110	13	0	1	2	14	24	16	6	2	.286/.445/.381
2016	COH	AAA	24	416	53	22	3	7	44	47	70	5	1	.325/.399/.461
2017	COH	AAA	25	374	56	17	1	5	33	60	56	1	2	.350/.454/.460
2017	CLE	MLB	25	179	25	8	1	0	13	21	35	2	0	.263/.352/.327
2018	COH	AAA	26	426	53	24	0	3	40	70	75	2	3	.293/.409/.388
2018	CLE	MLB	26	120	15	5	2	1	15	11	19	0	0	.312/.375/.422
2019	TBA	MLB	27	490	51	20	1	8	49	57	101	2	1	.263/.352/.371

Breakout: 9% Improve: 41% Collapse: 1% Attrition: 23% MLB: 70%
Comparables: Kevin Youkilis, Max Muncy, Eric Campbell

"Pretty" Yandy Diaz came into 2018 having crushed Triple-A two years in a row, and managed a high-OBP, low-power aria in the majors at the end of 2017. With Jason Kipnis' prime ending as abruptly as Bartolo's shave from Figaro, there was some hope he would take over at second base full time. Instead, despite another solid month of plate appearances, a closer look at the libretto shows he continued to blast the ball on the ground as hard as he could. Cleveland once again buried him in Triple-A despite Kipnis showing his collapse was here to stay. Yandy is a useful role player and deserving of an MLB roster spot, although despite his exit velocities, he's probably more of a beefed-up Eric Campbell rather than Jose Ramirez piu docile. When you hit the ball on the ground, no matter how hard you hit it, your reasonable best-case scenario is a single. His path to a starting job is now clear, thanks to a trade to Tampa Bay.

YEAR	TEAM	LVL	AGE	PA	DRC+	VORP	BABIP	BRR	FRAA	WARP
2016	AKR	AA	24	110	149	9.5	.328	-0.7	3B(22): -1.1, 2B(1): 0.0	0.5
2016	COH	AAA	24	416	148	28.9	.381	2.1	3B(30): -0.8, RF(28): 5.3	3.7
2017	COH	AAA	25	374	175	34.5	.412	1.1	3B(42): -3.4, LF(21): 0.7	3.4
2017	CLE	MLB	25	179	83	1.9	.336	-0.4	3B(40): -0.9, LF(3): -0.2	0.1
2018	COH	AAA	26	426	145	26.0	.360	-2.6	3B(73): -9.6, 1B(12): 0.2	1.5
2018	CLE	MLB	26	120	102	1.0	.371	-2.0	3B(9): 0.2, 1B(9): 0.2	0.1
2019	TBA	MLB	27	490	107	12.4	.325	-0.9	1B 1, 3B -1	1.4

Yandy Diaz, continued

Batted Ball Distribution

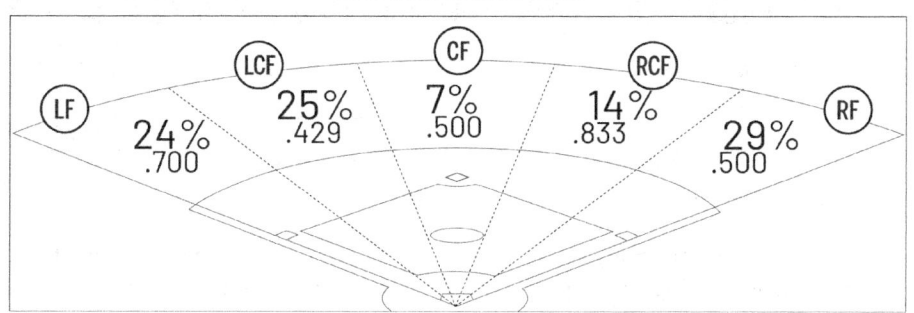

Strike Zone vs LHP   Strike Zone vs RHP

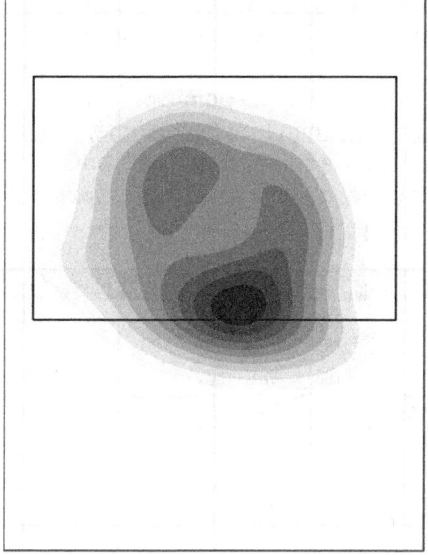

Matt Duffy   3B

Born: 01/15/91   Age: 28   Bats: R   Throws: R
Height: 6'2"   Weight: 170   Origin: Round 18, 2012 Draft (#568 overall)

YEAR	TEAM	LVL	AGE	PA	R	2B	3B	HR	RBI	BB	K	SB	CS	AVG/OBP/SLG
2016	SFN	MLB	25	286	32	11	2	4	21	20	40	8	4	.253/.313/.358
2016	TBA	MLB	25	80	9	3	0	1	7	3	13	0	1	.276/.300/.355
2018	TBA	MLB	27	560	59	22	1	4	44	47	93	12	6	.294/.361/.366
2019	TBA	MLB	28	470	49	20	2	6	44	40	79	9	4	.267/.337/.367

Breakout: 6%   Improve: 47%   Collapse: 6%   Attrition: 6%   MLB: 93%
Comparables: Chone Figgins, Josh Harrison, Freddy Sanchez

An uncertainty after missing all of 2017 with a foot injury, Duffy was the most steady hand in the Rays' lineup. He has terrific contact skills and rarely misses when he takes a swing. That said, his thin frame limits his power. He tallied just 27 extra-base hits in 560 trips to the plate and his career ISO is an even .100. His walk rate is around the league average and he's a decent runner, although his foot speed is lacking. When the Rays traded for Duffy in 2016, they intended for him to play shortstop. With better quick-twitch athletes on the roster, he was moved back to third base. He plays the position well and will make all of the routine plays, with a few out of his zone as well. Duffy is boring in the best way possible. At some point someone flashier with greater natural ability will challenge him for playing time, and perhaps Duffy will become more of a utility man as he creeps toward 30, but for now he's the least interesting man in Tampa Bay. Stay thirsty. Actually, Duffy would want you to be hydrated so he would bring you a water.

YEAR	TEAM	LVL	AGE	PA	DRC+	VORP	BABIP	BRR	FRAA	WARP
2016	SFN	MLB	25	286	84	10.0	.282	1.1	3B(69): 3.8	1.0
2016	TBA	MLB	25	80	87	0.8	.317	0.5	SS(18): 0.2, 3B(1): 0.0	0.3
2018	TBA	MLB	27	560	104	16.9	.353	-3.9	3B(125): 11.8, SS(1): 0.0	3.1
2019	TBA	MLB	28	470	98	9.8	.313	-0.2	3B 8	1.8

Matt Duffy, continued

Batted Ball Distribution

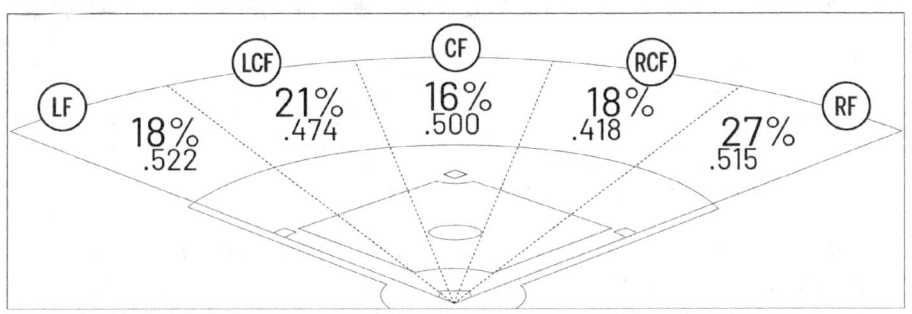

| **Strike Zone vs LHP** | **Strike Zone vs RHP** |

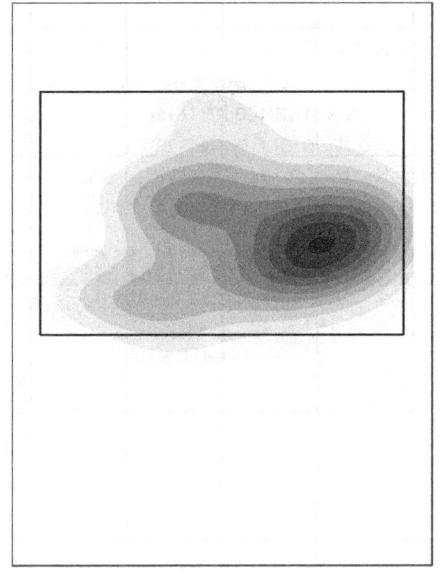 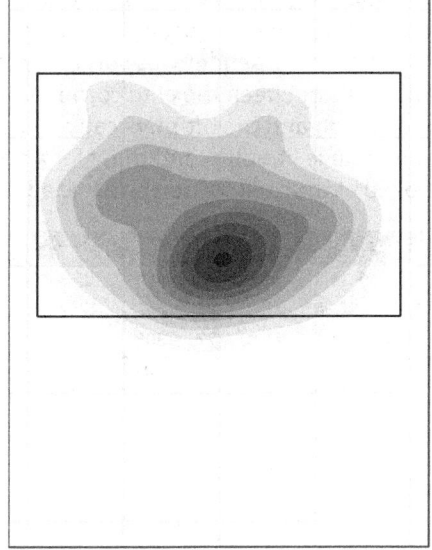

Avisail Garcia RF

Born: 06/12/91   Age: 28   Bats: R   Throws: R
Height: 6'4"   Weight: 240   Origin: International Free Agent, 2007

YEAR	TEAM	LVL	AGE	PA	R	2B	3B	HR	RBI	BB	K	SB	CS	AVG/OBP/SLG
2016	CHA	MLB	25	453	59	18	2	12	51	34	115	4	4	.245/.307/.385
2017	CHA	MLB	26	561	75	27	5	18	80	33	111	5	3	.330/.380/.506
2018	CHA	MLB	27	385	47	11	2	19	49	20	102	3	1	.236/.281/.438
2019	TBA	MLB	28	281	32	12	1	9	34	21	63	3	2	.264/.327/.425

Breakout: 3%   Improve: 48%   Collapse: 9%   Attrition: 11%   MLB: 99%
Comparables: Hunter Pence, Brennan Boesch, Delmon Young

The twinge Garcia felt in his right knee on Opening Day swiftly informed him that the follow-up to his All-Star breakout campaign would wind up landing somewhere between "unconventional," "troubled" and "downright hobbled." That trick knee would wind up taking the fall for inducing a pair of hamstring strains and persistent soreness, which conspired to limit Garcia to 93 games. There's no perfect accounting for how much a perturbed popliteal contributed to hampering a man who finished third in all of baseball in both infield hits and total batting average just a year before. But even with the knowledge that Garcia's tender bender was surgically repaired days after, pegging where his value falls between the elite corner outfielder performance he flashed in exactly one season and the oft-physically compromised mediocrity he's shown in his other four is literally something for an arbitrator to decide. The White Sox looked at that calculation and folded, opting instead to non-tender him.

YEAR	TEAM	LVL	AGE	PA	DRC+	VORP	BABIP	BRR	FRAA	WARP
2016	CHA	MLB	25	453	85	2.4	.309	2.0	RF(46): 6.1, LF(11): 0.0	0.8
2017	CHA	MLB	26	561	126	29.2	.392	-0.5	RF(132): 7.2	3.7
2018	CHA	MLB	27	385	98	4.3	.271	-1.4	RF(87): 6.3	1.2
2019	TBA	MLB	28	281	104	8.6	.317	-0.4	RF 2	1.0

Avisail Garcia, continued

Batted Ball Distribution

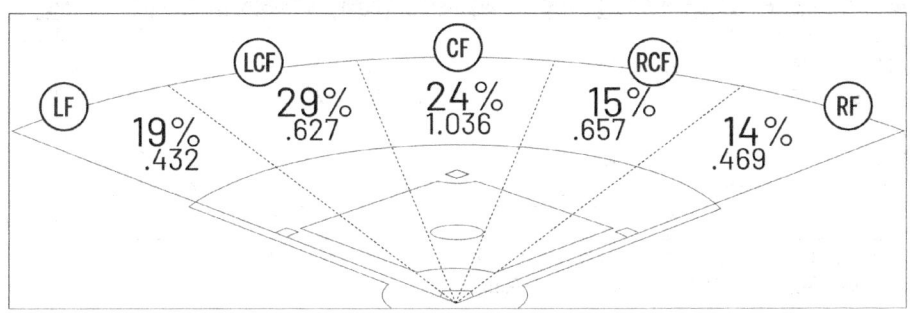

Strike Zone vs LHP **Strike Zone vs RHP**

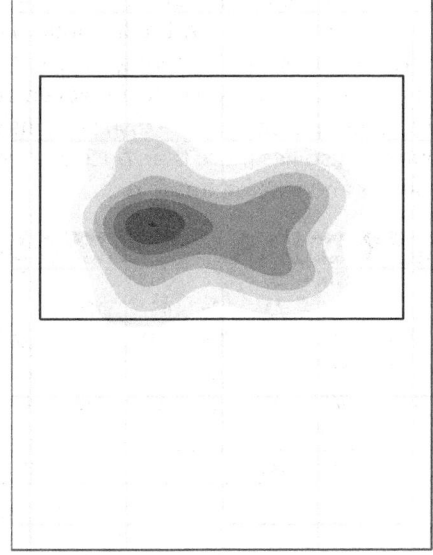

Guillermo Heredia LF

Born: 01/31/91   Age: 28   Bats: R   Throws: L
Height: 5'10"   Weight: 180   Origin: International Free Agent, 2016

YEAR	TEAM	LVL	AGE	PA	R	2B	3B	HR	RBI	BB	K	SB	CS	AVG/OBP/SLG
2016	WTN	AA	25	260	39	7	2	2	34	36	32	2	5	.293/.405/.376
2016	TAC	AAA	25	157	27	6	1	2	13	12	15	3	0	.312/.378/.413
2016	SEA	MLB	25	107	12	3	0	1	12	12	15	1	1	.250/.349/.315
2017	SEA	MLB	26	426	43	16	0	6	24	27	64	1	5	.249/.315/.337
2018	TAC	AAA	27	38	4	1	0	0	2	4	3	2	1	.276/.421/.310
2018	SEA	MLB	27	337	29	14	1	5	19	32	52	2	4	.236/.318/.342
2019	TBA	MLB	28	58	6	2	0	1	5	5	9	0	0	.235/.316/.333

Breakout: 1%   Improve: 44%   Collapse: 3%   Attrition: 16%   MLB: 91%
Comparables: Reggie Willits, David DeJesus, Aaron Hicks

Heredia is a joy to watch. His speed, accurate arm and route instincts made him one of the best outfielders in Seattle's organization. Unfortunately, at least until baseball legalizes a second designated hitter, he still has to get in a batter's box. It's there, after more than two years and 800 plate appearances in the big leagues, that things start to fall apart. Fully healed from a 2017 shoulder injury, Heredia got off to a blistering start, hitting .298/.417/.426 through the end of May. He couldn't keep it up, however, due primarily to a total lack of power. While his approach at the dish remains solid, unless he figures out how to punish mistakes more than once or twice a month he'll remain a fringe big leaguer and reserve outfielder.

YEAR	TEAM	LVL	AGE	PA	DRC+	VORP	BABIP	BRR	FRAA	WARP
2016	WTN	AA	25	260	138	17.7	.322	-1.0	CF(41): -2.8, RF(12): -0.1	0.9
2016	TAC	AAA	25	157	126	17.1	.333	2.1	CF(32): 0.6, LF(3): 0.1	1.0
2016	SEA	MLB	25	107	91	0.4	.289	-0.6	LF(35): 4.9, RF(14): -0.3	0.5
2017	SEA	MLB	26	426	88	2.3	.284	1.0	CF(63): 7.1, LF(62): 1.7	1.8
2018	TAC	AAA	27	38	113	4.9	.296	0.9	LF(6): 1.0, CF(5): -0.5	0.3
2018	SEA	MLB	27	337	89	8.1	.270	0.0	CF(89): -6.5, LF(32): 3.1	0.3
2019	TBA	MLB	28	58	77	0.5	.285	-0.2	CF 0, RF 1	0.0

Guillermo Heredia, continued

Batted Ball Distribution

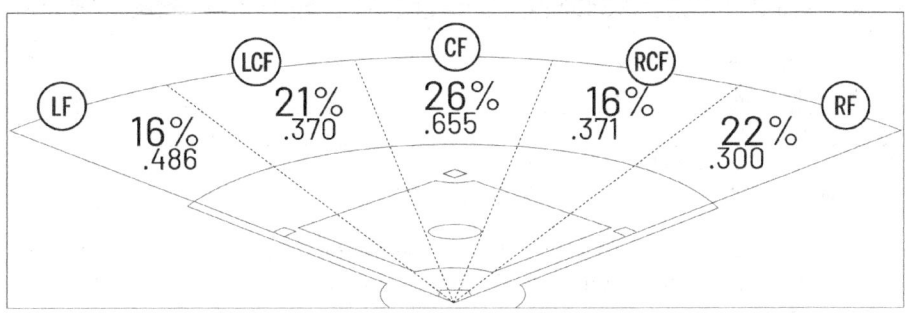

Strike Zone vs LHP   **Strike Zone vs RHP**

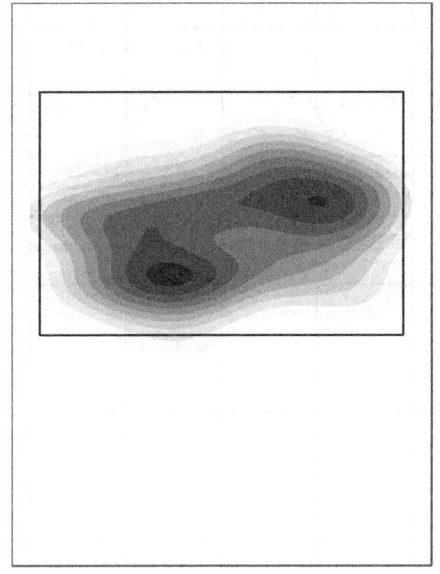 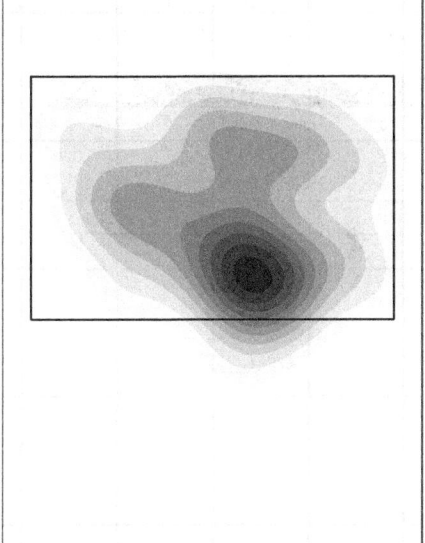

Kevin Kiermaier CF

Born: 04/22/90   Age: 29   Bats: L   Throws: R
Height: 6'1"   Weight: 215   Origin: Round 31, 2010 Draft (#941 overall)

YEAR	TEAM	LVL	AGE	PA	R	2B	3B	HR	RBI	BB	K	SB	CS	AVG/OBP/SLG
2016	TBA	MLB	26	414	55	20	2	12	37	40	74	21	3	.246/.331/.410
2017	TBA	MLB	27	421	56	15	3	15	39	31	99	16	7	.276/.338/.450
2018	TBA	MLB	28	367	44	12	9	7	29	25	91	10	5	.217/.282/.370
2019	TBA	MLB	29	506	68	20	6	13	49	41	111	18	6	.247/.317/.404

Breakout: 7%   Improve: 49%   Collapse: 11%   Attrition: 13%   MLB: 98%
Comparables: Angel Pagan, Franklin Gutierrez, Cameron Maybin

Kiermaier remains a spectacular defensive center fielder, with an argument for best-in-class status depending on whether Byron Buxton is still in the majors, but he's struggled to stay healthy and his offense took a step backward following a 2017 breakout. Under team control at reasonable salaries through 2023, he'll again anchor the Rays' defense while attempting to show that he can stay off the disabled list and out of the bottom of the lineup. Kiermaier is 28 years old and has cracked 500 plate appearances in a season just once, but few American League center fielders offer more potential for racking up WARP.

YEAR	TEAM	LVL	AGE	PA	DRC+	VORP	BABIP	BRR	FRAA	WARP
2016	TBA	MLB	26	414	99	18.3	.278	2.8	CF(104): 12.7	2.9
2017	TBA	MLB	27	421	101	24.6	.337	2.9	CF(97): 7.6	2.6
2018	TBA	MLB	28	367	76	6.4	.275	3.1	CF(88): 12.3	1.8
2019	TBA	MLB	29	506	96	20.3	.298	1.9	CF 10	2.9

Kevin Kiermaier, continued

Batted Ball Distribution

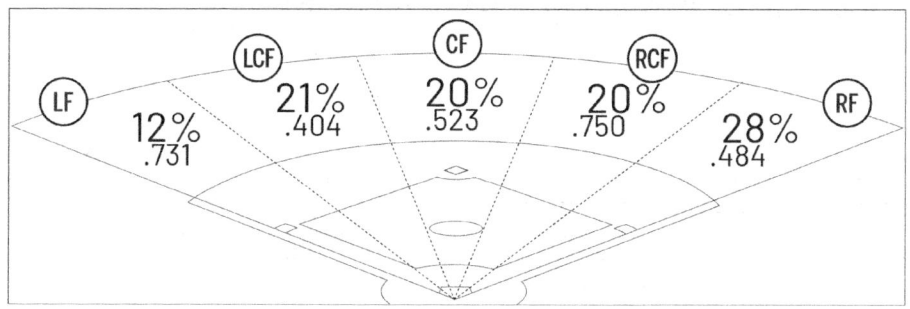

Strike Zone vs LHP   Strike Zone vs RHP

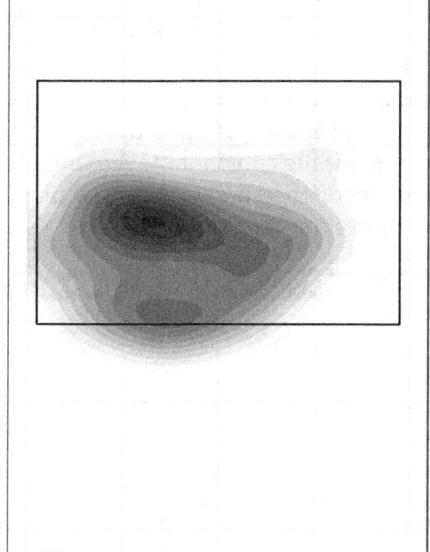

Brandon Lowe UT

Born: 07/06/94   Age: 24   Bats: L   Throws: R
Height: 6'0"   Weight: 185   Origin: Round 3, 2015 Draft (#87 overall)

YEAR	TEAM	LVL	AGE	PA	R	2B	3B	HR	RBI	BB	K	SB	CS	AVG/OBP/SLG
2016	BGR	A	21	449	67	15	3	5	42	60	77	6	3	.248/.357/.343
2017	PCH	A+	22	367	62	34	3	9	46	47	65	6	3	.311/.403/.524
2017	MNT	AA	22	101	8	5	1	2	12	2	26	1	1	.253/.270/.389
2018	MNT	AA	23	240	37	17	1	8	41	35	55	8	2	.291/.400/.508
2018	DUR	AAA	23	205	36	14	0	14	35	22	47	0	1	.304/.380/.613
2018	TBA	MLB	23	148	16	6	2	6	25	16	38	2	1	.233/.324/.450
2019	TBA	MLB	24	337	43	16	2	14	44	30	84	3	1	.243/.315/.449

Breakout: 12%   Improve: 43%   Collapse: 14%   Attrition: 34%   MLB: 75%
Comparables: Vince Belnome, Rob Refsnyder, Ryan Rua

A top-100 pick in 2015, Lowe broke out the boom stick in 2018 en route to the majors. Lowe hit just 16 home runs in his first 917 professional plate appearances, then smashed 28 in 593 trips to the plate last year across three levels, starting in Double-A and ending in the majors. In total, the former Maryland Terrapin collected a combined 68 extra-base hits during his three-city tour. The last six of his long balls came at the highest level, where he struggled to make contact when he was not mashing. Defensively, Lowe has split time between second base and the outfield corners. He's not particularly great at either, but the constant movement limits his exposure at each spot. A left-handed, offense-first, utility-type player with power is a profile out of which you can make a career.

YEAR	TEAM	LVL	AGE	PA	DRC+	VORP	BABIP	BRR	FRAA	WARP
2016	BGR	A	21	449	116	14.0	.298	-1.3	2B(88): -9.2	0.1
2017	PCH	A+	22	367	166	38.6	.366	2.0	2B(75): -1.1, 3B(2): -0.2	2.7
2017	MNT	AA	22	101	73	0.5	.319	-1.3	2B(24): 0.8	-0.3
2018	MNT	AA	23	240	158	25.7	.360	2.1	LF(26): 1.8, 2B(24): -3.2	1.7
2018	DUR	AAA	23	205	171	24.4	.339	0.4	2B(31): 1.2, LF(13): 0.9	2.1
2018	TBA	MLB	23	148	93	6.3	.279	0.8	2B(28): -0.6, LF(11): -0.3	0.3
2019	TBA	MLB	24	337	106	12.2	.289	-0.3	2B -1, RF -1	1.1

Brandon Lowe, continued

Batted Ball Distribution

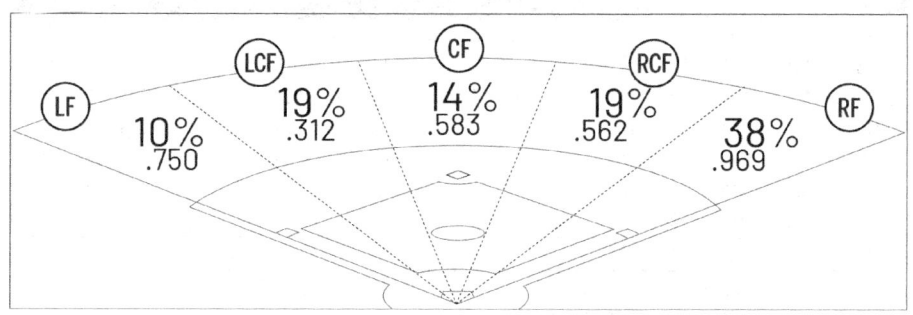

| **Strike Zone vs LHP** | **Strike Zone vs RHP** |

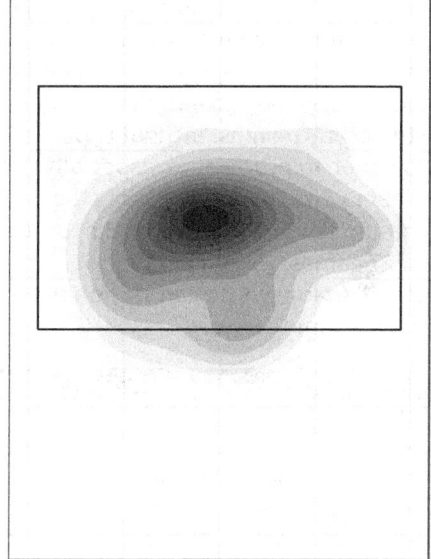

Austin Meadows OF

Born: 05/03/95 Age: 24 Bats: L Throws: L
Height: 6'3" Weight: 210 Origin: Round 1, 2013 Draft (#9 overall)

YEAR	TEAM	LVL	AGE	PA	R	2B	3B	HR	RBI	BB	K	SB	CS	AVG/OBP/SLG
2016	ALT	AA	21	190	33	16	8	6	23	16	32	9	3	.311/.365/.611
2016	IND	AAA	21	145	16	7	3	6	24	15	34	8	2	.214/.297/.460
2017	IND	AAA	22	312	48	19	0	4	36	24	50	11	3	.250/.311/.359
2018	IND	AAA	23	179	27	13	0	2	21	9	24	11	1	.279/.318/.394
2018	PIT	MLB	23	165	16	8	2	5	13	8	35	4	1	.292/.327/.468
2018	DUR	AAA	23	106	19	11	0	10	22	8	13	1	1	.344/.396/.771
2018	TBA	MLB	23	26	3	1	0	1	4	2	5	1	0	.250/.308/.417
2019	TBA	MLB	24	458	53	25	3	13	48	29	92	12	3	.223/.277/.390

Breakout: 11%   Improve: 51%   Collapse: 13%   Attrition: 19%   MLB: 87%
Comparables: Lewis Brinson, J.D. Martinez, Dalton Pompey

Once a shiny prospect, nagging injuries turned Meadows' profile into a matte finish heading into 2018. Some of the luster is back after the former top-10 pick appeared in a career-high 128 games, including the first 59 contests of his big-league career. Seemingly trapped behind Andrew McCutchen for a few seasons, both outfielders left Pittsburgh behind in 2018 and actually ended the year as AL East rivals. Meadows has hit at every stop along the way and continued to do so in the bigs. The most intriguing part of his season was his power moving from projection to production, especially following the mid-July trade that sent Chris Archer to Pittsburgh. In leading the Durham Bulls to an International League championship, Meadows smashed 21 extra-base hits, including 10 home runs, in just 27 games. He can hit. He can hit for power now. He can run and he can defend. As long as he can stay on the field, Meadows will be a key piece of the up-and-coming Rays.

YEAR	TEAM	LVL	AGE	PA	DRC+	VORP	BABIP	BRR	FRAA	WARP
2016	ALT	AA	21	190	150	19.7	.343	0.8	CF(39): 2.5, LF(2): -0.5	1.6
2016	IND	AAA	21	145	92	9.6	.236	0.9	CF(23): -3.1, LF(11): -0.2	-0.1
2017	IND	AAA	22	312	92	9.0	.289	3.7	CF(33): -1.9, LF(24): -0.8	0.3
2018	IND	AAA	23	179	150	8.3	.314	2.4	CF(22): -1.5, LF(18): 0.1	1.3
2018	PIT	MLB	23	165	95	8.0	.345	-1.1	CF(15): -0.7, RF(13): -1.1	0.1
2018	DUR	AAA	23	106	147	15.0	.311	-1.6	CF(17): -1.2, RF(4): -0.2	0.4
2018	TBA	MLB	23	26	95	0.4	.278	-0.1	RF(7): -1.4, LF(1): 0.0	-0.1
2019	TBA	MLB	24	458	76	1.6	.252	1.4	RF -7, LF 1	-0.5

Austin Meadows, continued

Batted Ball Distribution

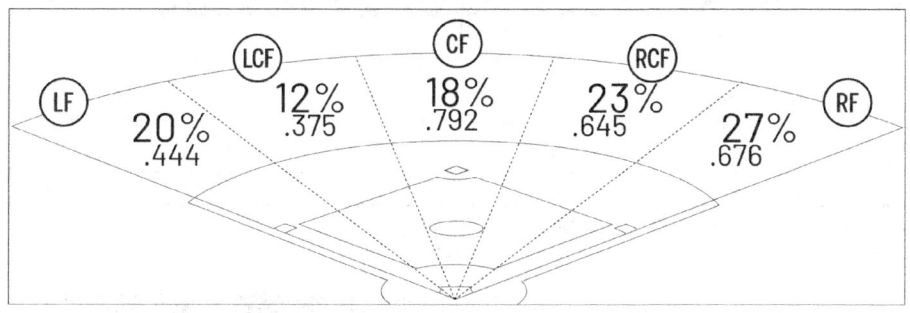

Strike Zone vs LHP   **Strike Zone vs RHP**

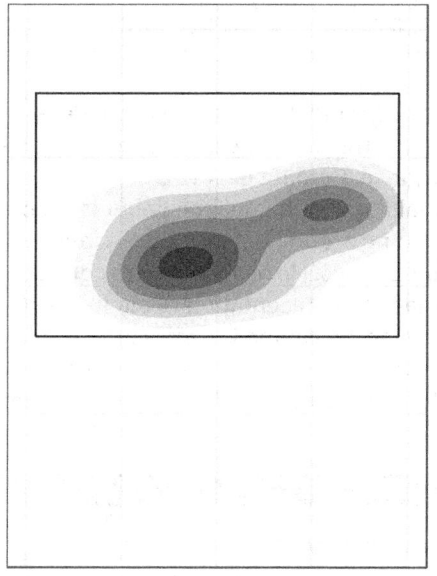 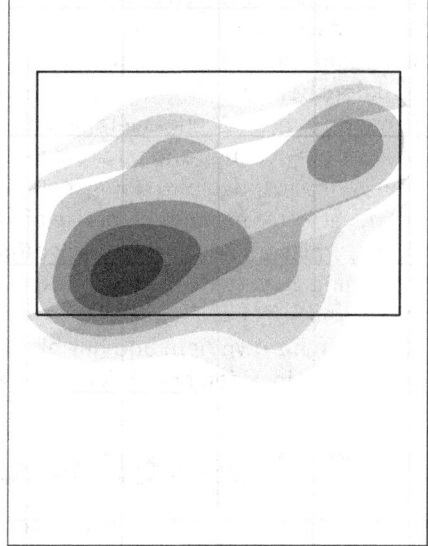

Michael Perez C

Born: 08/07/92 Age: 26 Bats: L Throws: R
Height: 5'11" Weight: 180 Origin: Round 5, 2011 Draft (#154 overall)

YEAR	TEAM	LVL	AGE	PA	R	2B	3B	HR	RBI	BB	K	SB	CS	AVG/OBP/SLG
2016	MOB	AA	23	131	7	4	1	3	10	7	29	0	1	.205/.252/.328
2016	VIS	A+	23	173	17	10	2	1	19	15	33	1	0	.256/.318/.365
2017	WTN	AA	24	302	29	23	0	5	39	35	61	0	2	.279/.365/.424
2018	RNO	AAA	25	240	30	9	1	6	29	20	40	0	1	.284/.342/.417
2018	TBA	MLB	25	80	9	5	0	1	11	3	19	0	0	.284/.304/.392
2019	TBA	MLB	26	147	15	5	1	4	16	11	32	0	0	.239/.299/.381

Breakout: 8%   Improve: 28%   Collapse: 6%   Attrition: 26%   MLB: 51%
Comparables: Bryan Holaday, Bryan Anderson, Chris Herrmann

Perez was acquired at the trade deadline in exchange for Matt Andriese and almost instantly became the club's starting catcher. A left-handed hitter, he has blossomed at the plate over the past two seasons in the minors and showed similar ability in the majors before falling victim to a hamstring injury late in the season. Perez just needs to be a league-average bat to make this work, because he draws rave reviews from coaches and pitchers for his glove. Coming over to a new organization is tough and doing it while making your big-league debut is even harder, yet Perez earned the praise of everyone around him. He's quick and athletic, which allows him to block difficult pitches. He has the arm to control the running game and quiet hands to manage the presentation of pitches. The time share with Mike Zunino will be interesting, as Zunino is a tremendous defender in his own right and has big-time power. A strict platoon does not appear to be in order, but look for Perez to hold his own while vying for playing time.

YEAR	TEAM	P. COUNT	FRM RUNS	BLK RUNS	THRW RUNS	TOT RUNS
2017	WTN	9926	2.4	3.5	0.1	6.6
2018	RNO	8459	2.6	1.6	0.8	5.1
2018	TBA	2989	-3.5	0.5	0.0	-2.5
2019	TBA	5486	-2.0	1.0	0.0	-1.0

YEAR	TEAM	LVL	AGE	PA	DRC+	VORP	BABIP	BRR	FRAA	WARP
2016	MOB	AA	23	131	58	-0.1	.242	0.3	C(36): 5.2	0.4
2016	VIS	A+	23	173	78	5.2	.315	-1.0	C(47): 3.0	0.2
2017	WTN	AA	24	302	133	16.7	.343	-1.8	C(73): 7.4	2.5
2018	RNO	AAA	25	240	98	10.2	.322	-1.3	C(57): 8.7	1.6
2018	TBA	MLB	25	80	88	2.2	.357	-1.8	C(24): -3.6	-0.3
2019	TBA	MLB	26	147	85	4.0	.284	-0.2	C -1	0.3

Michael Perez, continued

Batted Ball Distribution

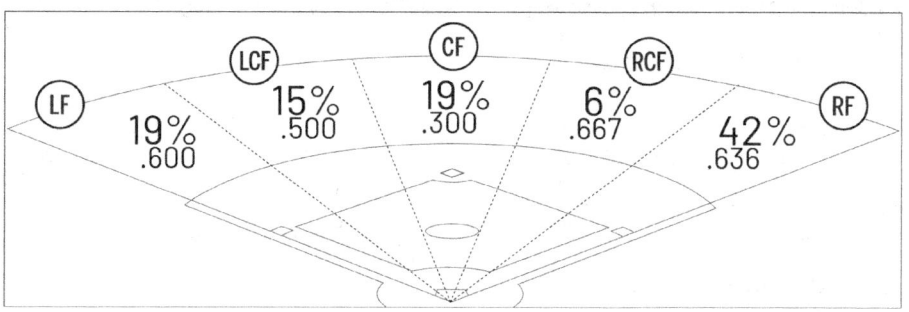

Strike Zone vs LHP   Strike Zone vs RHP

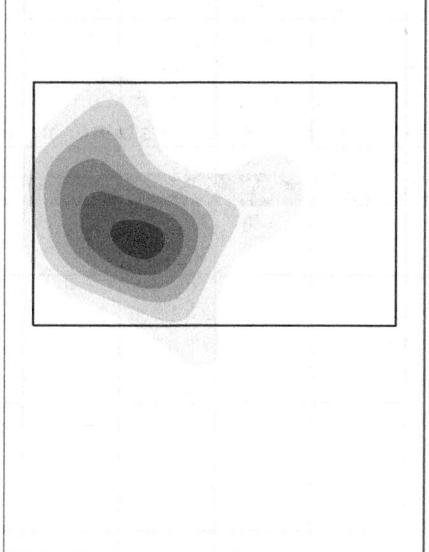

Tommy Pham LF

Born: 03/08/88 Age: 31 Bats: R Throws: R
Height: 6'1" Weight: 210 Origin: Round 16, 2006 Draft (#496 overall)

YEAR	TEAM	LVL	AGE	PA	R	2B	3B	HR	RBI	BB	K	SB	CS	AVG/OBP/SLG
2016	MEM	AAA	28	128	15	5	1	3	17	18	29	8	2	.236/.344/.382
2016	SLN	MLB	28	183	26	7	0	9	17	20	71	2	2	.226/.324/.440
2017	MEM	AAA	29	106	17	8	0	4	19	13	21	6	3	.283/.371/.500
2017	SLN	MLB	29	530	95	22	2	23	73	71	117	25	7	.306/.411/.520
2018	SLN	MLB	30	396	67	11	0	14	41	42	97	10	6	.248/.331/.399
2018	TBA	MLB	30	174	35	7	6	7	22	25	43	5	1	.343/.448/.622
2019	TBA	MLB	31	585	85	23	3	20	64	67	150	18	7	.251/.346/.427

Breakout: 1% Improve: 32% Collapse: 14% Attrition: 10% MLB: 94%
Comparables: Luke Scott, Chris Dickerson, Carlos Beltran

The Rays essentially took a flier on Pham at the trade deadline, acquiring him for useful but still spare pieces of the farm system. Off to a slow start with the Cardinals after a 2017 breakout, Pham rewarded his new club with a torrid second half. After playing considerable time in center field with St. Louis, he will not be receiving many reps there with the Rays, but is playable in left field. Pham will be 31 on Opening Day and doesn't really fit in with the Rays' younger nucleus. However, he's team controllable through his prime and should be the leader of a lineup that gets better around him as he ages.

YEAR	TEAM	LVL	AGE	PA	DRC+	VORP	BABIP	BRR	FRAA	WARP
2016	MEM	AAA	28	128	104	7.1	.295	1.9	CF(24): -2.8, LF(4): 0.2	0.1
2016	SLN	MLB	28	183	83	7.7	.342	0.7	CF(34): -2.1, LF(30): -2.3	-0.2
2017	MEM	AAA	29	106	130	9.3	.328	0.7	RF(15): 2.2, CF(9): -1.0	0.7
2017	SLN	MLB	29	530	140	58.0	.368	4.6	LF(86): -2.6, CF(37): 0.1	4.3
2018	SLN	MLB	30	396	122	18.3	.303	3.8	CF(91): -5.1	2.3
2018	TBA	MLB	30	174	121	21.4	.442	0.9	LF(37): -0.5, CF(3): -0.2	0.9
2019	TBA	MLB	31	585	112	31.7	.311	0.8	LF -3, CF -3	2.3

Tommy Pham, continued

Batted Ball Distribution

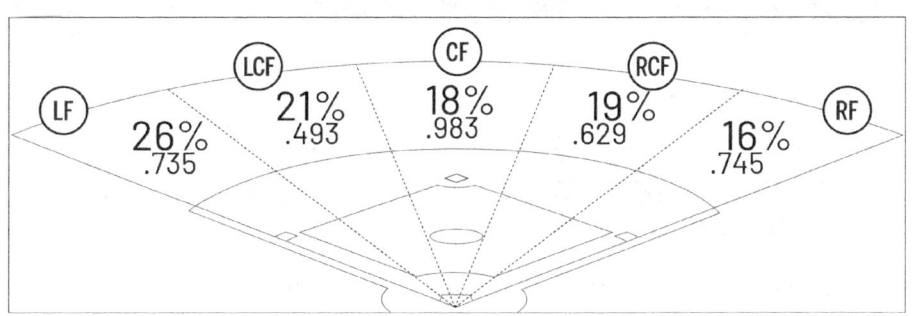

Strike Zone vs LHP   Strike Zone vs RHP

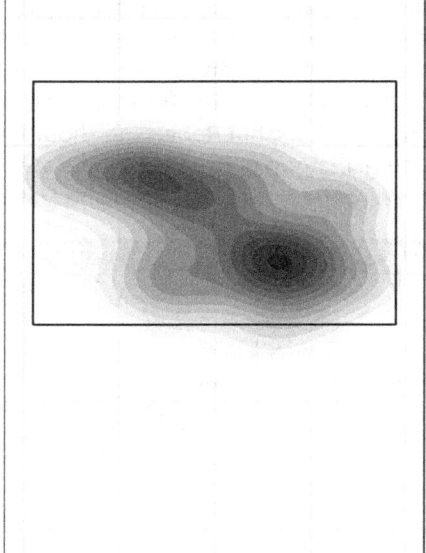

Daniel Robertson UT

Born: 03/22/94 Age: 25 Bats: R Throws: R
Height: 5'11" Weight: 200 Origin: Round 1, 2012 Draft (#34 overall)

YEAR	TEAM	LVL	AGE	PA	R	2B	3B	HR	RBI	BB	K	SB	CS	AVG/OBP/SLG
2016	DUR	AAA	22	511	50	21	3	5	43	58	100	2	1	.259/.358/.356
2017	DUR	AAA	23	47	7	2	0	1	1	3	7	0	1	.372/.426/.488
2017	TBA	MLB	23	254	22	7	2	5	19	29	73	1	1	.206/.308/.326
2018	TBA	MLB	24	340	46	16	0	9	34	43	77	2	2	.262/.382/.415
2019	TBA	MLB	25	438	45	16	1	10	45	45	103	2	1	.228/.320/.354

Breakout: 13% Improve: 61% Collapse: 4% Attrition: 16% MLB: 100%
Comparables: Dustin Ackley, Luis Valbuena, Nick Franklin

The 34th selection in the 2012 draft and a former top-100 prospect, Robertson has carved out a role as the 10th man for Tampa Bay. After rising through the ranks as a shortstop, he entered the season as the Rays' primary backup to the four, five and six spots. He also pitched, played first base and made a handful of starts in left field. Robertson's defensive flexibility is useful, but it was his bat that emerged as the biggest part of his value before a thumb injury ended his season in August. Prior to the ailment, Robertson continued a tremendous aptitude for walks and increased power from the right side. He was on his way to a two-WARP season, finishing just short. The Rays have plenty of reserve infield options, but Robertson should remain the club's top choice, as he's a natural platoon with Joey Wendle at second base along with his ability to back up Willy Adames at shortstop and Matt Duffy at third base.

YEAR	TEAM	LVL	AGE	PA	DRC+	VORP	BABIP	BRR	FRAA	WARP
2016	DUR	AAA	22	511	109	18.5	.322	-0.3	SS(75): 1.7, 2B(21): 2.1	2.4
2017	DUR	AAA	23	47	138	3.3	.429	-1.0	SS(4): 0.3, 3B(3): -0.2	0.3
2017	TBA	MLB	23	254	79	1.4	.282	-0.8	2B(41): -2.2, SS(24): 1.9	0.2
2018	TBA	MLB	24	340	112	24.9	.328	1.8	2B(39): 3.1, SS(29): -0.3	2.1
2019	TBA	MLB	25	438	93	9.0	.284	-0.8	SS 1, 3B 0	1.0

Daniel Robertson, continued

Batted Ball Distribution

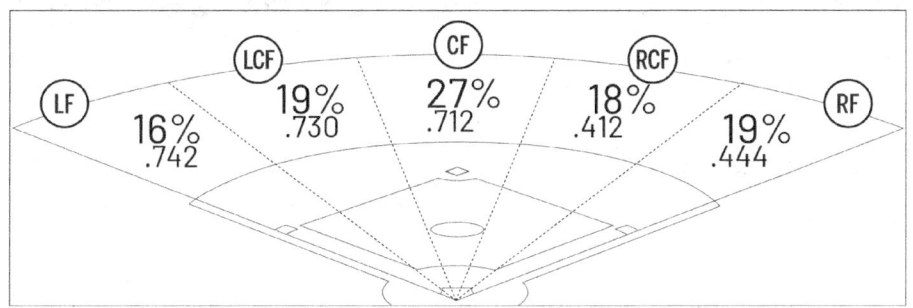

Strike Zone vs LHP **Strike Zone vs RHP**

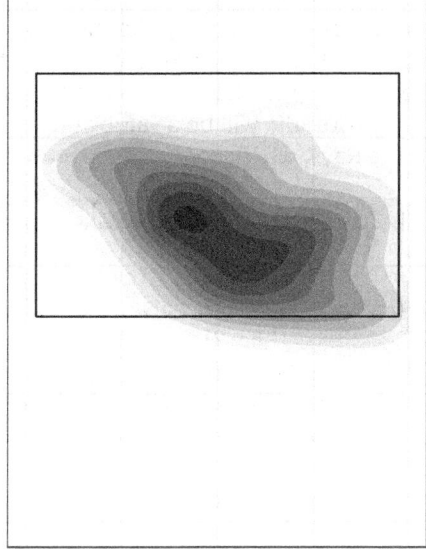

Joey Wendle 2B

Born: 04/26/90 Age: 29 Bats: L Throws: R
Height: 6'1" Weight: 190 Origin: Round 6, 2012 Draft (#203 overall)

YEAR	TEAM	LVL	AGE	PA	R	2B	3B	HR	RBI	BB	K	SB	CS	AVG/OBP/SLG
2016	NAS	AAA	26	526	81	31	9	12	61	26	112	14	4	.279/.324/.452
2016	OAK	MLB	26	104	11	1	0	1	11	6	16	2	0	.260/.298/.302
2017	NAS	AAA	27	510	67	29	8	8	54	19	82	13	4	.285/.327/.429
2017	OAK	MLB	27	14	3	1	0	1	5	1	3	0	0	.308/.357/.615
2018	TBA	MLB	28	545	62	33	6	7	61	37	96	16	4	.300/.354/.435
2019	TBA	MLB	29	512	53	27	6	10	54	28	103	11	3	.257/.309/.403

Breakout: 6% Improve: 22% Collapse: 13% Attrition: 23% MLB: 57%
Comparables: Mike Fontenot, Whit Merrifield, Jason Donald

Wendle made quite the impression in 2018 in his first extended look at the top level. He was a steady hand defensively at second base, but also filled in at shortstop, third base and both corner outfield spots. That he's a multi-faceted defender is not much of a shock. The fact that he was an offensive force who racked up over 40 extra-base hits and was on base 35 percent of the time was a huge surprise, especially after his *2018 Annual* comment called for a 2049 breakout. Even with some regression—he maintained a high BABIP without elite speed and opposing pitchers may question the sustainability of his power—Wendle will be a value at the keystone. The late break is actually great for the Rays, who'll control him through his prime.

YEAR	TEAM	LVL	AGE	PA	DRC+	VORP	BABIP	BRR	FRAA	WARP
2016	NAS	AAA	26	526	96	25.4	.340	3.2	2B(122): 4.7	1.2
2016	OAK	MLB	26	104	92	0.5	.296	-0.7	2B(28): 1.5	0.3
2017	NAS	AAA	27	510	96	26.3	.329	0.6	2B(82): -0.7, 3B(24): 6.3	1.4
2017	OAK	MLB	27	14	93	1.0	.333	-0.2	2B(5): -0.5	0.0
2018	TBA	MLB	28	545	108	33.8	.353	3.7	2B(100): 5.8, 3B(20): 1.4	3.2
2019	TBA	MLB	29	512	92	14.3	.306	1.2	2B 5, 3B 1	2.0

Joey Wendle, continued

Batted Ball Distribution

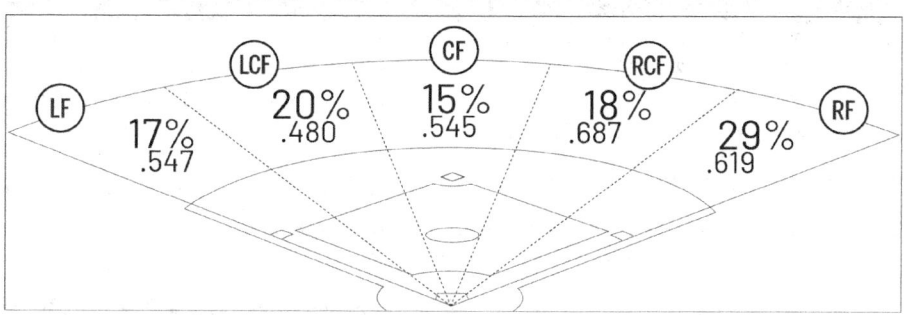

Strike Zone vs LHP   **Strike Zone vs RHP**

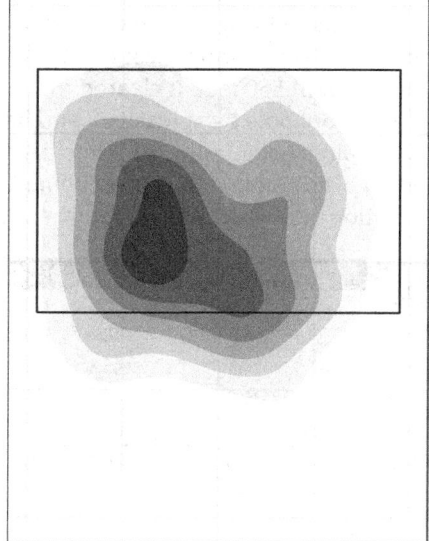

Mike Zunino   C

Born: 03/25/91   Age: 28   Bats: R   Throws: R
Height: 6'2"   Weight: 220   Origin: Round 1, 2012 Draft (#3 overall)

YEAR	TEAM	LVL	AGE	PA	R	2B	3B	HR	RBI	BB	K	SB	CS	AVG/OBP/SLG
2016	TAC	AAA	25	327	47	15	0	17	57	35	69	0	1	.286/.376/.521
2016	SEA	MLB	25	192	16	7	0	12	31	21	65	0	0	.207/.318/.470
2017	TAC	AAA	26	45	7	2	0	5	11	4	5	0	0	.293/.356/.707
2017	SEA	MLB	26	435	52	25	0	25	64	39	160	1	0	.251/.331/.509
2018	SEA	MLB	27	405	37	18	0	20	44	24	150	0	0	.201/.259/.410
2019	TBA	MLB	28	411	49	18	1	17	52	34	130	0	0	.226/.300/.418

Breakout: 6%   Improve: 43%   Collapse: 15%   Attrition: 10%   MLB: 94%
Comparables: Jarrod Saltalamacchia, J.P. Arencibia, Yan Gomes

On April 21, 2014, Houston Astros reliever Chad Qualls tried to throw Mike Zunino a sinker down. He missed thigh high, and Zunino squared it up. The result was a ball hit so far that, had it been hit back in the days before television, your grandpa would have sworn it went 550 feet. It cleared the left-field foul pole by at least 30, and banged off the outer wall of Safeco Field. The umpires got together and decided the ball had hooked foul. It was the perfect distillation of the Mike Zunino Offensive Experience, a jaw-dropping exhibition of raw strength and power. It was also a strike.

YEAR	TEAM	P. COUNT	FRM RUNS	BLK RUNS	THRW RUNS	TOT RUNS
2016	SEA	6955	3.0	1.6	-0.2	3.9
2017	SEA	16181	10.9	-3.1	-0.6	5.6
2017	TAC	823	1.0	0.0	0.0	0.9
2018	SEA	14630	7.5	-1.1	0.4	6.6
2019	TBA	15337	9.2	-1.1	-0.2	7.9

YEAR	TEAM	LVL	AGE	PA	DRC+	VORP	BABIP	BRR	FRAA	WARP
2016	TAC	AAA	25	327	144	29.7	.318	-2.5	C(57): 17.9	3.8
2016	SEA	MLB	25	192	109	12.6	.250	-1.7	C(52): 3.7	1.4
2017	TAC	AAA	26	45	151	9.0	.226	0.6	C(7): 0.8	0.5
2017	SEA	MLB	26	435	109	27.8	.355	-1.4	C(120): 6.3	3.1
2018	SEA	MLB	27	405	83	6.5	.268	-2.2	C(111): 6.4	1.6
2019	TBA	MLB	28	411	98	16.9	.294	-0.8	C 5	2.1

Mike Zunino, continued

Batted Ball Distribution

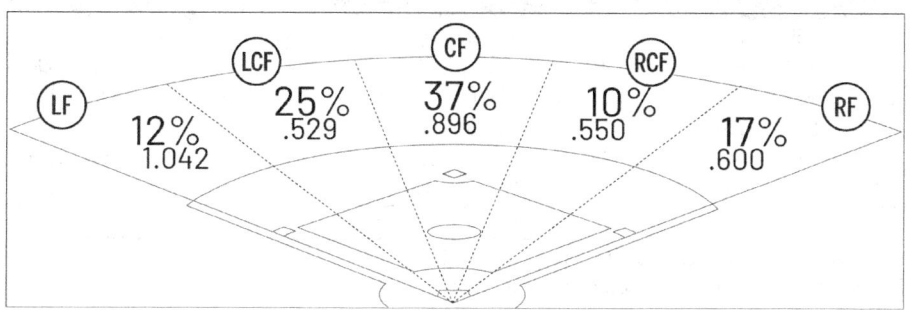

Strike Zone vs LHP   **Strike Zone vs RHP**

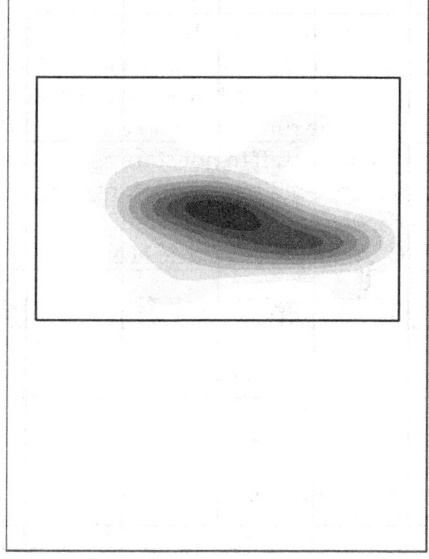

Jose Alvarado LHP

Born: 05/21/95   Age: 24   Bats: L   Throws: L
Height: 6'2"   Weight: 245   Origin: International Free Agent, 2012

YEAR	TEAM	LVL	AGE	W	L	SV	G	GS	IP	H	HR	BB/9	K/9	K	GB%	BABIP
2016	BGR	A	21	2	0	2	10	0	24^2	12	0	6.2	12.4	34	74%	.245
2016	PCH	A+	21	2	1	0	27	0	46	38	1	7.4	10.0	51	57%	.306
2017	MNT	AA	22	2	1	0	9	0	11^1	4	1	4.0	11.1	14	78%	.136
2017	DUR	AAA	22	0	2	1	16	0	18^1	11	1	6.4	12.8	26	43%	.244
2017	TBA	MLB	22	0	3	0	35	0	29^2	24	1	2.7	8.8	29	55%	.274
2018	TBA	MLB	23	1	6	8	70	0	64	42	1	4.1	11.2	80	57%	.270
2019	TBA	MLB	24	3	3	22	64	0	67	51	5	5.8	11.0	83	52%	.287

Breakout: 27%   Improve: 57%   Collapse: 18%   Attrition: 24%   MLB: 91%
Comparables: Aroldis Chapman, Dominic Leone, Josh Spence

Big, burly and left-handed, Alvarado has all the pieces to be a late-inning weapon for years to come. Signed out of Maracaibo, Venezuela in 2012, he converted to a relief role in 2016. Despite never pitching above rookie-ball before that, he was in the majors a year later and doing serious damage to opposing batters in 2018. Going more with a sinker/slider combination over a four-seam/curveball approach, he struck out 80 batters in 64 innings. His upper-90s heater allowed him to keep the ball close to the ground with just a single home run allowed to the 263 batters he faced. One of the few members of the pitching staff to not start or open a game, he did, however, make an appearance at first base before going back to the mound in a matchup bonanza. He converted eight saves and is a candidate for more as the back-end of the Rays' bullpen lacks a true ace.

YEAR	TEAM	LVL	AGE	WHIP	ERA	DRA	WARP	MPH	FB%	WHF	CSP
2016	BGR	A	21	1.18	1.46	2.45	0.7				
2016	PCH	A+	21	1.65	3.91	3.57	0.8				
2017	MNT	AA	22	0.79	2.38	2.41	0.3				
2017	DUR	AAA	22	1.31	3.93	2.93	0.5				
2017	TBA	MLB	22	1.11	3.64	3.44	0.6	99.7	75.8	11.5	48.3
2018	TBA	MLB	23	1.11	2.39	2.65	1.7	99.3	70.5	13.6	49
2019	TBA	MLB	24	1.40	3.44	3.97	0.9	99.2	74	13.4	50.1

Jose Alvarado, continued

Pitch Shape vs LHH

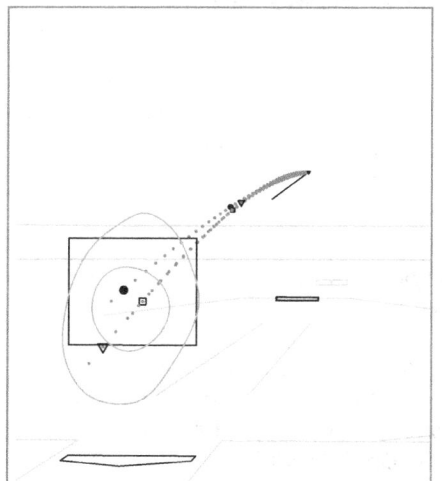

Pitch Shape vs RHH

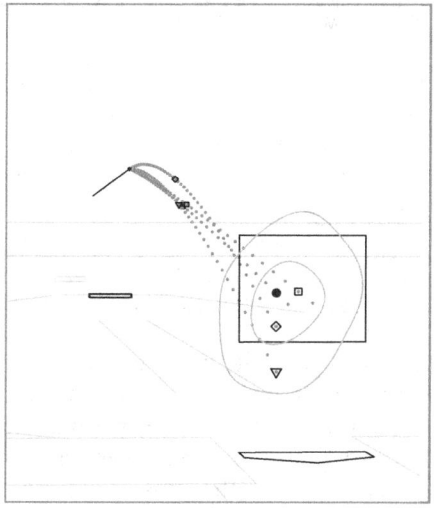

Type	Frequency	Velocity	H Movement	V Movement
● Fastball	13.7%	97.9 [117]	5.5 [105]	-13.2 [108]
□ Sinker	56.8%	98 [128]	11.6 [108]	-14.7 [119]
+ Cutter				
▲ Changeup				
× Splitter				
▽ Slider	18.9%	88.4 [117]	-2.2 [88]	-33 [100]
◇ Curveball	10.6%	84.1 [121]	-1.4 [73]	-41.8 [114]
⊕ Slow Curveball				
✷ Knuckleball				
▼ Screwball				

Rays Player Analysis - 53

Jalen Beeks LHP

Born: 07/10/93   Age: 25   Bats: L   Throws: L
Height: 5'11"   Weight: 195   Origin: Round 12, 2014 Draft (#374 overall)

YEAR	TEAM	LVL	AGE	W	L	SV	G	GS	IP	H	HR	BB/9	K/9	K	GB%	BABIP
2016	SLM	A+	22	4	4	0	13	13	67^1	67	9	3.2	7.4	55	43%	.294
2016	PME	AA	22	5	4	0	13	13	65^1	72	6	3.9	7.7	56	35%	.330
2017	PME	AA	23	5	1	0	9	9	49^1	35	3	4.0	10.6	58	51%	.276
2017	PAW	AAA	23	6	7	0	17	17	95^2	86	10	3.1	9.1	97	45%	.291
2018	BOS	MLB	24	0	1	0	2	1	6^1	11	1	5.7	7.1	5	33%	.435
2018	PAW	AAA	24	5	5	0	16	16	87^1	70	10	2.6	12.1	117	41%	.299
2018	TBA	MLB	24	5	0	0	12	0	44^1	41	5	4.1	7.5	37	51%	.288
2019	TBA	MLB	25	4	4	0	29	10	70^1	63	8	3.7	9.2	72	42%	.293

Breakout: 13%   Improve: 36%   Collapse: 22%   Attrition: 41%   MLB: 70%
Comparables: Manny Parra, Eric Surkamp, Wade Miley

Acquired in a trade that actually benefited both teams, Beeks swapped AL East clubs with Nathan Eovaldi, who would help the Red Sox win the whole damn thing a few months later. Beeks has years of team control left and a skill set that fits the organization's new take on pitching. On the shorter side without tremendous stuff, the Rays used Beeks a dozen times for an average of about three-and-a-half innings per outing. Only 11 times did he pitch to a batter three times in the same game as a reliever, protecting him from the third-time-through-the-order penalty. After switching sides, he increased the use of his changeup while throwing fewer fastballs. Whether or not the opener remains a thing, Tampa Bay will likely continue to use multi-inning relievers, which means Beeks should be in the plans for the foreseeable future.

YEAR	TEAM	LVL	AGE	WHIP	ERA	DRA	WARP	MPH	FB%	WHF	CSP
2016	SLM	A+	22	1.35	3.07	4.14	1.0				
2016	PME	AA	22	1.53	4.68	4.07	0.8				
2017	PME	AA	23	1.16	2.19	3.90	0.7				
2017	PAW	AAA	23	1.24	3.86	4.25	1.5				
2018	BOS	MLB	24	2.37	12.79	7.48	-0.2	93.5	47.5	9.5	42.7
2018	PAW	AAA	24	1.09	2.89	3.71	1.8				
2018	TBA	MLB	24	1.38	4.47	5.18	-0.1	93.5	47.5	13.1	45
2019	TBA	MLB	25	1.30	3.85	4.33	0.8	93.2	48.6	12.8	45.7

Jalen Beeks, continued

Pitch Shape vs LHH

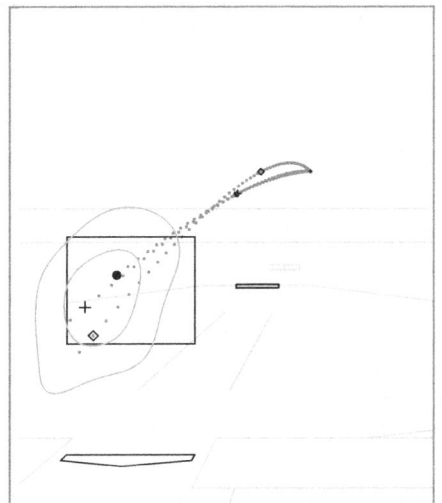

Pitch Shape vs RHH

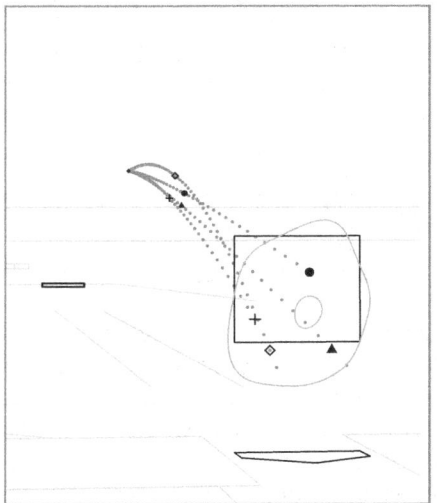

Type	Frequency	Velocity	H Movement	V Movement
● Fastball	42.7%	92.2 [99]	7.2 [98]	-14 [105]
□ Sinker	0.6%	93.6 [106]	12.4 [101]	-15.6 [115]
+ Cutter	19.7%	87.5 [93]	-0.7 [93]	-23.6 [100]
▲ Changeup	18.3%	87.3 [108]	14.9 [81]	-26.9 [101]
× Splitter				
▽ Slider				
◇ Curveball	18.8%	77.2 [95]	-10.3 [110]	-52.4 [90]
⊕ Slow Curveball				
✳ Knuckleball				
▼ Screwball				

Diego Castillo RHP

Born: 01/18/94   Age: 25   Bats: R   Throws: R
Height: 6'3"   Weight: 240   Origin: International Free Agent, 2014

YEAR	TEAM	LVL	AGE	W	L	SV	G	GS	IP	H	HR	BB/9	K/9	K	GB%	BABIP
2016	BGR	A	22	1	3	7	24	0	40	34	1	2.5	11.2	50	49%	.317
2016	PCH	A+	22	2	3	3	14	0	20[1]	28	3	2.7	7.5	17	52%	.357
2017	MNT	AA	23	1	3	8	21	0	29	20	1	2.2	9.9	32	61%	.250
2017	DUR	AAA	23	3	2	7	30	1	42[2]	38	2	2.7	12.2	58	40%	.353
2018	DUR	AAA	24	0	1	4	19	0	26[1]	15	1	2.4	10.9	32	59%	.246
2018	TBA	MLB	24	4	2	0	43	11	56[2]	36	6	2.9	10.3	65	46%	.229
2019	TBA	MLB	25	3	3	12	51	6	59	50	6	3.6	10.0	66	45%	.292

Breakout: 26%   Improve: 44%   Collapse: 18%   Attrition: 35%   MLB: 73%
Comparables: Yimi Garcia, Jerry Blevins, Sam Tuivailala

Castillo, a traditional reliever since turning professional in 2014, started in 11 of his 43 appearances as part of the opener movement. He was effective in either role, limiting the opposition to a .206/.231/.333 line when beginning a game and a .166/.261/.288 mark when following a teammate. He used a conventional two-pitch mix, working primarily off an upper-90s fastball and a slider that tickled 90 as well, striking out 29 percent of batters faced. The slider is particularly effective, as he used the pitch to complete 53 of his 65 strikeouts and it held opponents to a .106 average. Despite the absence of a changeup, Castillo held his own against left-handed batters, though his control waned at times. His comfort level in any role makes him a key asset going into 2019.

YEAR	TEAM	LVL	AGE	WHIP	ERA	DRA	WARP	MPH	FB%	WHF	CSP
2016	BGR	A	22	1.12	2.03	2.18	1.2				
2016	PCH	A+	22	1.67	4.87	3.17	0.4				
2017	MNT	AA	23	0.93	1.86	2.49	0.8				
2017	DUR	AAA	23	1.20	3.38	2.27	1.4				
2018	DUR	AAA	24	0.84	1.03	1.90	1.0				
2018	TBA	MLB	24	0.95	3.18	3.70	0.9	100.5	54	14	48.9
2019	TBA	MLB	25	1.25	3.33	3.85	0.9	100.2	55.3	14.3	50.1

Diego Castillo, continued

Pitch Shape vs LHH

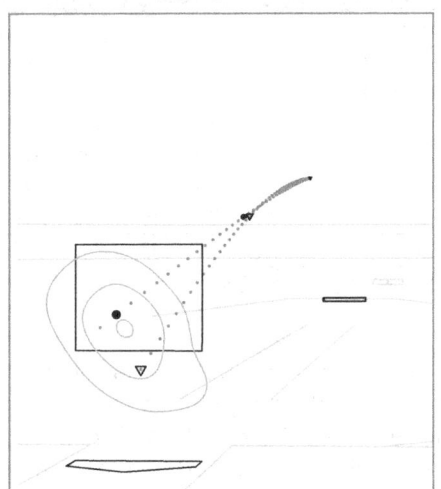

Pitch Shape vs RHH

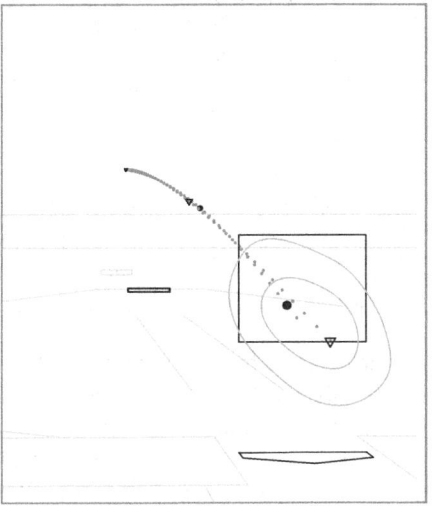

Type	Frequency	Velocity	H Movement	V Movement
● Fastball	51.4%	98 [118]	-12.1 [75]	-17.3 [95]
☐ Sinker	2.6%	99.8 [137]	-14.2 [87]	-15.8 [115]
+ Cutter				
▲ Changeup				
✕ Splitter				
▽ Slider	46.0%	89.3 [122]	5.1 [101]	-28.2 [114]
◇ Curveball				
⊕ Slow Curveball				
✳ Knuckleball				
▼ Screwball				

Rays Player Analysis - 57

Yonny Chirinos   RHP

Born: 12/26/93   Age: 25   Bats: R   Throws: R
Height: 6'2"   Weight: 235   Origin: International Free Agent, 2012

YEAR	TEAM	LVL	AGE	W	L	SV	G	GS	IP	H	HR	BB/9	K/9	K	GB%	BABIP
2016	BGR	A	22	1	0	0	4	2	11^2	8	0	0.8	6.9	9	56%	.222
2016	PCH	A+	22	6	1	0	11	7	50^1	47	5	0.5	5.5	31	53%	.262
2016	MNT	AA	22	5	3	0	14	8	66^2	74	5	1.6	5.8	43	44%	.307
2017	MNT	AA	23	1	0	0	4	4	27^1	22	5	1.3	6.9	21	58%	.233
2017	DUR	AAA	23	12	5	0	23	22	141	116	10	1.4	7.7	120	52%	.270
2018	DUR	AAA	24	0	2	0	8	8	30^2	35	7	2.1	9.1	31	50%	.326
2018	TBA	MLB	24	5	5	0	18	7	89^2	84	7	2.5	7.5	75	45%	.298
2019	TBA	MLB	25	3	3	0	10	10	50	49	7	2.6	7.6	42	45%	.292

Breakout: 12%   Improve: 38%   Collapse: 24%   Attrition: 33%   MLB: 83%
Comparables: A.J. Griffin, Tim Cooney, Jose Urena

Chirinos signed for a modest $10,000 out of Venezuela in 2012. He methodically worked his way through the system, culminating with being named the organization's minor-league pitcher of the year in 2017 and making his big-league debut in 2018. He spent the majority of his time as a starter in the minors and started seven games for Tampa Bay, but was mostly used as a bulk guy. In 11 relief appearances he racked up 57 1/3 innings and was highly effective, limiting the other team to a .276 wOBA and a strikeout-to-walk ratio of 3.5:1. Born in '93, his heavy fastball mimics his birth year. Even with modest velocity, the pitch was relatively effective in setting up a hard slider and a particularly damaging split-finger. The mid-80s offering was the catalyst in most of his strikeouts. Chirinos has the build and pitch mix to start games at the highest level. He did miss about a month with a forearm injury, but was highly effective down the stretch.

YEAR	TEAM	LVL	AGE	WHIP	ERA	DRA	WARP	MPH	FB%	WHF	CSP
2016	BGR	A	22	0.77	2.31	3.52	0.2				
2016	PCH	A+	22	0.99	2.15	3.14	1.3				
2016	MNT	AA	22	1.29	4.45	3.42	1.3				
2017	MNT	AA	23	0.95	2.63	3.55	0.5				
2017	DUR	AAA	23	0.98	2.74	3.27	3.7				
2018	DUR	AAA	24	1.37	5.28	4.70	0.3				
2018	TBA	MLB	24	1.22	3.51	4.23	0.9	95.9	63.1	12.2	49.8
2019	TBA	MLB	25	1.27	4.09	4.63	0.5	95.6	64.6	12.5	50.9

Yonny Chirinos, continued

Pitch Shape vs LHH

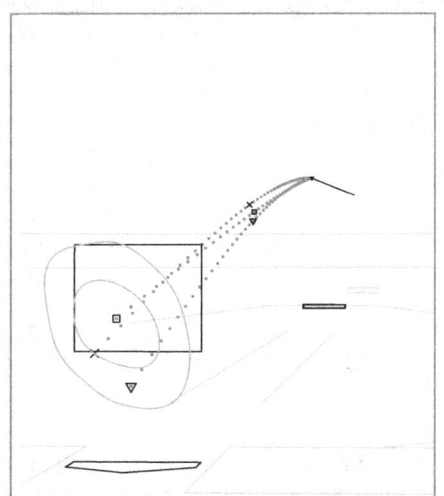

Pitch Shape vs RHH

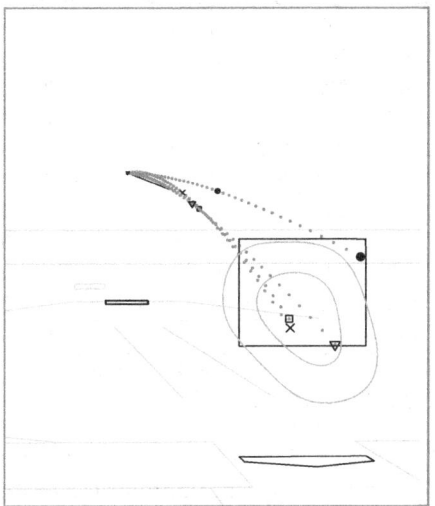

Type	Frequency	Velocity	H Movement	V Movement
● Fastball	5.8%	94.9 [108]	-6.1 [103]	-12.5 [110]
□ Sinker	57.3%	94.2 [108]	-14.3 [86]	-18.5 [106]
+ Cutter				
▲ Changeup				
× Splitter	14.8%	86 [102]	-5.5 [110]	-30.8 [95]
▽ Slider	22.1%	88.3 [117]	2.1 [88]	-25.9 [121]
◇ Curveball				
⊕ Slow Curveball				
✳ Knuckleball				
▼ Screwball				

Rays Player Analysis - 59

Oliver Drake RHP

Born: 01/13/87   Age: 32   Bats: R   Throws: R
Height: 6'4"   Weight: 215   Origin: Round 43, 2008 Draft (#1286 overall)

YEAR	TEAM	LVL	AGE	W	L	SV	G	GS	IP	H	HR	BB/9	K/9	K	GB%	BABIP
2016	NOR	AAA	29	1	4	10	47	1	56.1	44	5	4.0	12.6	79	46%	.322
2016	BAL	MLB	29	1	0	0	14	0	18	11	2	3.5	10.5	21	52%	.205
2017	BAL	MLB	30	0	0	0	3	0	3.1	6	0	8.1	8.1	3	67%	.500
2017	MIL	MLB	30	3	5	1	61	0	52.2	57	6	3.8	10.1	59	49%	.349
2018	MIL	MLB	31	1	0	0	11	0	12.2	14	0	5.7	10.7	15	57%	.400
2018	CLE	MLB	31	0	0	0	4	0	4.1	7	0	2.1	8.3	4	31%	.438
2018	SLC	AAA	31	0	0	0	6	0	7.2	3	0	1.2	9.4	8	71%	.176
2018	ANA	MLB	31	0	1	0	8	0	8.2	15	2	1.0	8.3	8	39%	.448
2018	TOR	MLB	31	0	0	0	2	0	1.2	4	0	0.0	10.8	2	43%	.571
2018	MIN	MLB	31	0	0	0	19	0	20.1	12	2	3.1	9.7	22	55%	.204
2019	TBA	MLB	32	1	1	0	13	0	13	13	2	4.0	9.1	14	47%	.297

Breakout: 22%   Improve: 40%   Collapse: 15%   Attrition: 18%   MLB: 69%
Comparables: Jason Bulger, Mitch Stetter, Blake Wood

The thing is, Drake is actually pretty good. Pitching is hard enough. To pitch in the majors requires supernal sheer arm strength, tremendous proprioception, a very high tolerance for pain and a sharp intellect. To pitch in the majors for five different teams in a single season requires all those things, plus considerable mental toughness. It requires that five teams decide you're good enough to merit a roster spot, but it also requires four of them to decide some other fringe player is better. As most difficult tasks do, however, pitching becomes easier when one makes it simple and focuses on their strengths. In Drake's case, that finally happened when he reached Minnesota in early August. From his arrival there through the end of the season, he threw his splitter (almost a true forkball, and easily his best offering) more often than any other pitch. Opponents batted .164/.238/.274 against Drake down the stretch. May he never go back to throwing the heater more often than the split. At the time this book went to print, Drake was already on his second team of 2019, which puts him on pace to have worn every jersey in the league by late summer.

YEAR	TEAM	LVL	AGE	WHIP	ERA	DRA	WARP	MPH	FB%	WHF	CSP
2016	NOR	AAA	29	1.22	2.72	2.07	1.9				
2016	BAL	MLB	29	1.00	4.00	2.86	0.4	92.3	54.2	15.6	49.5
2017	BAL	MLB	30	2.70	8.10	6.84	-0.1	92.9	47.6	11	43.7
2017	MIL	MLB	30	1.50	4.44	4.35	0.5	93.5	51.6	13	45.1
2018	MIL	MLB	31	1.74	6.39	2.52	0.4	93.9	49.3	13.5	50.5
2018	CLE	MLB	31	1.85	12.46	2.59	0.1	93.7	48.1	14.3	45.6
2018	SLC	AAA	31	0.52	1.17	3.56	0.1				
2018	ANA	MLB	31	1.85	5.19	3.11	0.2	94.2	47.1	15	49.1
2018	TOR	MLB	31	2.40	16.20	1.95	0.1	94.1	58.3	8.3	52.2
2018	MIN	MLB	31	0.93	2.21	3.40	0.4	93.7	40.6	13.6	45.5
2019	*TBA*	*MLB*	*32*	*1.41*	*3.99*	*4.44*	*0.1*	*92.6*	*48.6*	*13.3*	*46.8*

Tampa Bay Rays 2019

Oliver Drake, continued

Pitch Shape vs LHH

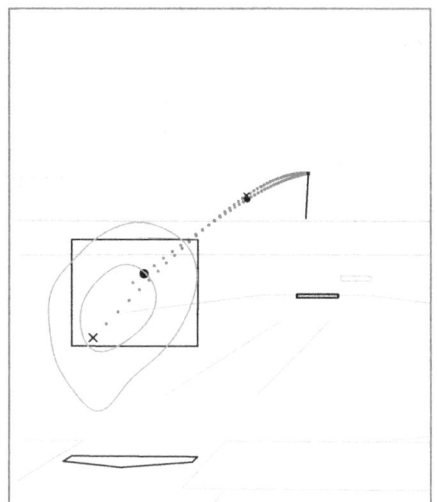

Pitch Shape vs RHH

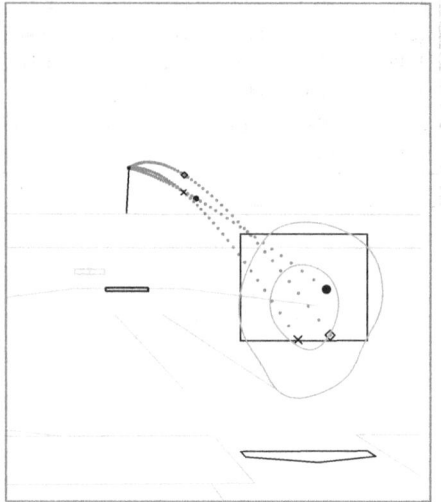

Type	Frequency	Velocity	H Movement	V Movement
● Fastball	45.6%	93 [102]	0.5 [133]	-11.9 [112]
□ Sinker				
+ Cutter				
▲ Changeup				
× Splitter	41.5%	84.4 [93]	-4.3 [115]	-30.2 [97]
▽ Slider	2.0%	84.6 [101]	1.8 [87]	-30.6 [107]
◇ Curveball	10.9%	80.6 [108]	1.7 [74]	-46.5 [103]
⊕ Slow Curveball				
✳ Knuckleball				
▼ Screwball				

Jacob Faria RHP

Born: 07/30/93 Age: 25 Bats: R Throws: R
Height: 6'4" Weight: 235 Origin: Round 10, 2011 Draft (#330 overall)

YEAR	TEAM	LVL	AGE	W	L	SV	G	GS	IP	H	HR	BB/9	K/9	K	GB%	BABIP
2016	MNT	AA	22	1	6	0	14	14	83^1	64	5	3.9	10.0	93	42%	.282
2016	DUR	AAA	22	4	4	0	13	13	67^2	46	7	4.3	8.5	64	40%	.227
2017	DUR	AAA	23	6	1	0	11	11	58^2	44	7	3.4	12.9	84	43%	.291
2017	TBA	MLB	23	5	4	0	16	14	86^2	71	11	3.2	8.7	84	39%	.265
2018	DUR	AAA	24	2	1	0	7	5	29^1	25	5	4.0	8.6	28	38%	.253
2018	TBA	MLB	24	4	4	0	17	12	65	60	9	4.6	6.9	50	35%	.274
2019	TBA	MLB	25	4	4	0	23	10	70	66	10	4.2	8.2	64	39%	.285

Breakout: 16%   Improve: 56%   Collapse: 23%   Attrition: 28%   MLB: 91%
Comparables: Ian Kennedy, Rubby De La Rosa, Chris Archer

At a time when velocity runs the yard, Faria remains the zig to the zag, with a low-90s fastball leading the way. He was a productive member of the rotation as a rookie in 2017, but 2018 was a net negative. After beginning the season as one of the few regular members of the Rays' rotation, he missed about two-and-a-half months with an oblique strain and was not particularly sharp before or after the injury. Faria wasn't necessarily a control artist coming through the system, but had a good feel for the zone in 2017, walking fewer than nine percent of batters. That number jumped up in 2018, with a drop in strikeouts. He especially struggled going against the platoon split, walking more lefties (25) than he struck out (24). Not surprisingly, his changeup was one of the big reasons for his issues. Briefly demoted in August before finishing the season in the majors, he allowed more runs than innings pitched in September.

YEAR	TEAM	LVL	AGE	WHIP	ERA	DRA	WARP	MPH	FB%	WHF	CSP
2016	MNT	AA	22	1.20	4.21	3.56	1.5				
2016	DUR	AAA	22	1.15	3.72	5.98	-0.5				
2017	DUR	AAA	23	1.12	3.07	3.28	1.6				
2017	TBA	MLB	23	1.18	3.43	4.33	1.2	93.1	54.5	13.3	46.3
2018	DUR	AAA	24	1.30	4.60	5.38	0.0				
2018	TBA	MLB	24	1.43	5.40	6.75	-1.1	93.0	60.6	8.8	47.1
2019	TBA	MLB	25	1.37	4.59	5.09	0.2	92.8	58.9	11.3	47.9

Jacob Faria, continued

Pitch Shape vs LHH

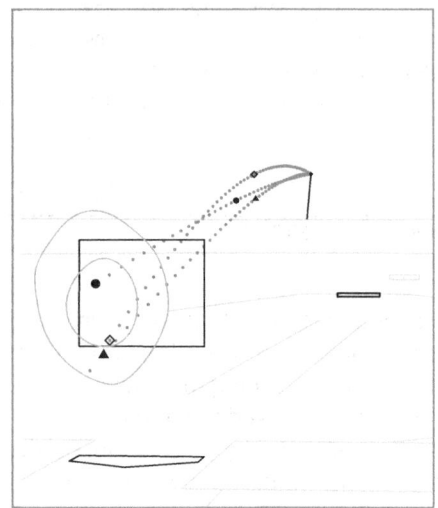

Pitch Shape vs RHH

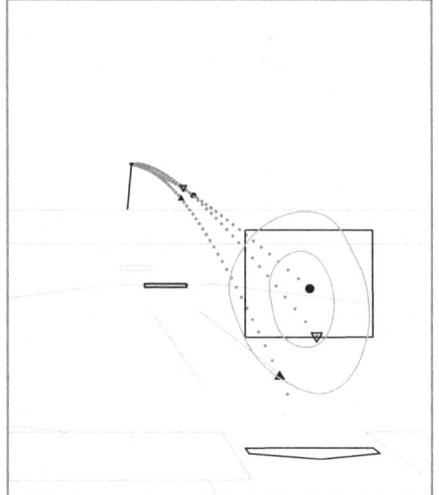

Type	Frequency	Velocity	H Movement	V Movement
● Fastball	60.6%	92.2 [99]	-1 [126]	-12.9 [109]
☐ Sinker				
+ Cutter				
▲ Changeup	18.6%	81.7 [86]	-7.6 [120]	-32.3 [85]
✕ Splitter				
▽ Slider	17.7%	83.7 [96]	4.1 [97]	-32.2 [102]
◇ Curveball	3.1%	76 [91]	5 [88]	-50 [96]
⊕ Slow Curveball				
✳ Knuckleball				
▼ Screwball				

Tyler Glasnow RHP

Born: 08/23/93 Age: 25 Bats: L Throws: R
Height: 6'8" Weight: 220 Origin: Round 5, 2011 Draft (#152 overall)

YEAR	TEAM	LVL	AGE	W	L	SV	G	GS	IP	H	HR	BB/9	K/9	K	GB%	BABIP
2016	IND	AAA	22	8	3	0	20	20	110^2	65	4	5.0	10.8	133	43%	.255
2016	PIT	MLB	22	0	2	0	7	4	23^1	22	2	5.0	9.3	24	49%	.317
2017	IND	AAA	23	9	2	0	15	15	93^1	57	6	3.1	13.5	140	50%	.276
2017	PIT	MLB	23	2	7	0	15	13	62	81	13	6.4	8.1	56	44%	.358
2018	PIT	MLB	24	1	2	0	34	0	56	47	5	5.5	11.6	72	57%	.321
2018	TBA	MLB	24	1	5	0	11	11	55^2	42	10	3.1	10.3	64	44%	.248
2019	TBA	MLB	25	9	8	0	26	26	130	106	11	4.7	10.4	150	46%	.290

Breakout: 34% Improve: 63% Collapse: 17% Attrition: 21% MLB: 92%
Comparables: Edinson Volquez, Carlos Marmol, Gio Gonzalez

During a year in which the Rays seemingly turned every starter into a reliever and every reliever into a starter, Glasnow, acquired as part of the deadline return for Chris Archer, was allowed to return to his old ways in the rotation. After focusing on trying to get the ball down in Pittsburgh, Glasnow worked higher in the zone for Tampa Bay. Predictably, the result was more fly balls and more home runs, but also fewer pitches out of the zone and easier outs on balls in play. The 6-foot-8 righty made 11 starts for Tampa Bay down the stretch and was able to maintain velocity and effectiveness with the increased workload. He projects to be the club's no. 2 starter behind Blake Snell and has breakout potential.

YEAR	TEAM	LVL	AGE	WHIP	ERA	DRA	WARP	MPH	FB%	WHF	CSP
2016	IND	AAA	22	1.15	1.87	3.80	2.0				
2016	PIT	MLB	22	1.50	4.24	4.40	0.2	96.8	62.3	12.2	43.7
2017	IND	AAA	23	0.95	1.93	2.58	3.2				
2017	PIT	MLB	23	2.02	7.69	8.17	-1.8	97.4	64.7	8.6	46.9
2018	PIT	MLB	24	1.45	4.34	2.88	1.4	99.2	72.5	12.4	46.3
2018	TBA	MLB	24	1.10	4.20	3.64	0.9	98.8	68.2	13.2	48.5
2019	TBA	MLB	25	1.33	3.55	4.02	2.1	98.1	69.6	11.7	47.4

Tyler Glasnow, continued

Pitch Shape vs LHH

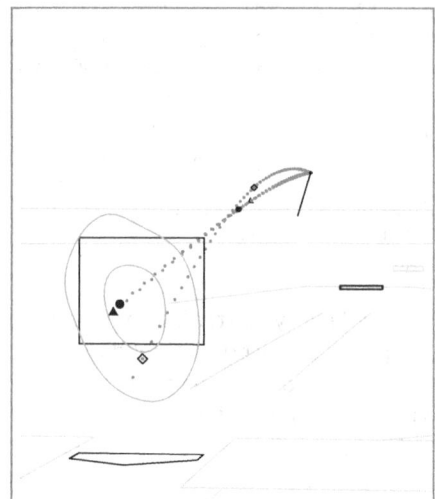

Pitch Shape vs RHH

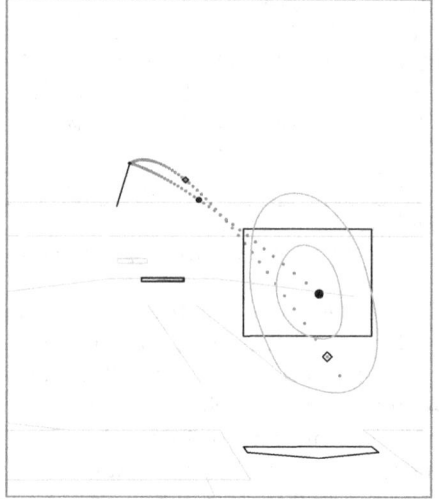

Type	Frequency	Velocity	H Movement	V Movement
● Fastball	70.5%	97.3 [115]	1.1 [136]	-12.9 [109]
☐ Sinker				
+ Cutter				
▲ Changeup	1.7%	92.4 [128]	-9.3 [111]	-21.4 [118]
✕ Splitter				
▽ Slider	1.1%	85.5 [105]	4.8 [100]	-43.6 [69]
◇ Curveball	26.6%	83.9 [120]	5.3 [89]	-48 [100]
⊕ Slow Curveball				
✱ Knuckleball				
▼ Screwball				

Charlie Morton RHP

Born: 11/12/83   Age: 35   Bats: R   Throws: R
Height: 6'5"   Weight: 235   Origin: Round 3, 2002 Draft (#95 overall)

YEAR	TEAM	LVL	AGE	W	L	SV	G	GS	IP	H	HR	BB/9	K/9	K	GB%	BABIP
2016	PHI	MLB	32	1	1	0	4	4	17^1	15	1	4.2	9.9	19	66%	.326
2017	HOU	MLB	33	14	7	0	25	25	146^2	125	14	3.1	10.0	163	53%	.295
2018	HOU	MLB	34	15	3	0	30	30	167	130	18	3.4	10.8	201	49%	.284
2019	TBA	MLB	35	10	8	0	26	26	148	126	13	3.8	9.7	160	51%	.296

Breakout: 13%   Improve: 40%   Collapse: 27%   Attrition: 13%   MLB: 89%
Comparables: Ryan Dempster, Chuck Finley, Jeff Fassero

Morton may be the best proof that the Astros are operating on a level above most teams. His career health record reads like the script for a *Grey's Anatomy* episode, and he entered free agency two offseasons ago best known not for his own success, but for imitating the late, great Roy Halladay's mound mannerisms. We'd tagged him as an "inconsistent no. 4 starter" before the 2016 season, and then he barely pitched before he tore his hamstring. Despite all of that, the Astros quickly snapped Morton up for $14 million over two years. He returned their act of faith with the two most effective and healthy seasons of his or most careers, sustaining a large velocity spike to go along with a now-untouchable curveball. He even closed out Game 7 of the 2017 World Series with four electric innings out of the bullpen. Credit great analytics, scouting, coaching and preventative health, because you need all of it working in harmony to turn Charlie Morton into a borderline ace. Tampa Bay will now attempt to recreate the magic, this time for $30 million over two years.

YEAR	TEAM	LVL	AGE	WHIP	ERA	DRA	WARP	MPH	FB%	WHF	CSP
2016	PHI	MLB	32	1.33	4.15	3.11	0.4	96.5	61.6	13	44.7
2017	HOU	MLB	33	1.19	3.62	3.92	2.7	96.6	65.6	11.5	48.6
2018	HOU	MLB	34	1.16	3.13	3.68	3.1	97.5	63.4	12.8	48.3
2019	TBA	MLB	35	1.28	3.49	3.96	2.5	95.8	63.1	12.1	46.6

Tampa Bay Rays 2019

Charlie Morton, continued

Pitch Shape vs LHH

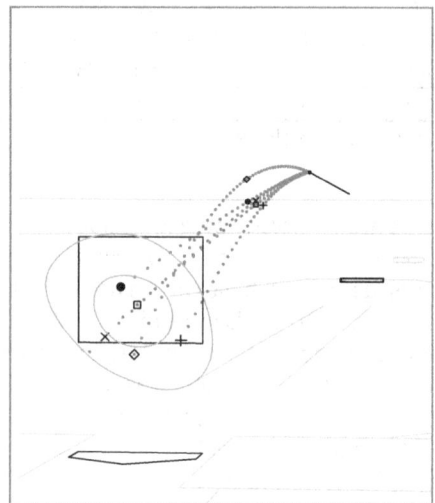

Pitch Shape vs RHH

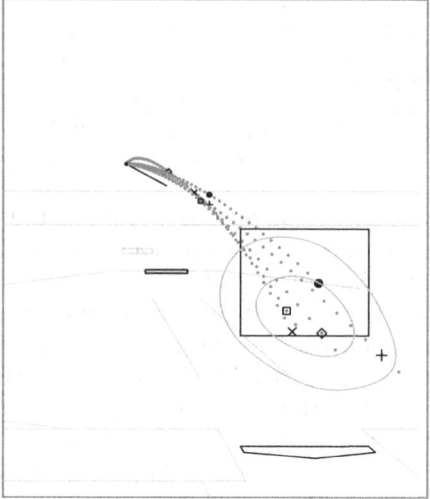

Type	Frequency	Velocity	H Movement	V Movement
● Fastball	29.2%	96.6 [113]	-11.9 [76]	-15.4 [101]
□ Sinker	29.1%	95.6 [116]	-14.7 [82]	-20.9 [98]
+ Cutter	5.2%	89.2 [102]	3.2 [108]	-26.5 [89]
▲ Changeup	0.2%	87.4 [108]	-16.1 [74]	-29.6 [93]
× Splitter	6.0%	87.7 [111]	-15.9 [70]	-28.8 [103]
▽ Slider	1.0%	86.7 [110]	5.3 [102]	-32.3 [102]
◇ Curveball	29.3%	80 [106]	16.1 [135]	-48.6 [99]
⊕ Slow Curveball				
✳ Knuckleball				
▼ Screwball				

Emilio Pagan   RHP

Born: 05/07/91   Age: 28   Bats: L   Throws: R
Height: 6'3"   Weight: 210   Origin: Round 10, 2013 Draft (#297 overall)

YEAR	TEAM	LVL	AGE	W	L	SV	G	GS	IP	H	HR	BB/9	K/9	K	GB%	BABIP
2016	WTN	AA	25	4	1	9	18	0	30²	19	1	3.2	13.2	45	32%	.269
2016	TAC	AAA	25	1	2	1	23	0	34¹	28	6	4.7	10.2	39	32%	.268
2017	TAC	AAA	26	2	1	5	23	0	31²	19	0	2.3	10.2	36	29%	.241
2017	SEA	MLB	26	2	3	0	34	0	50¹	39	7	1.4	10.0	56	23%	.258
2018	NAS	AAA	27	1	0	0	5	0	6	5	2	0.0	16.5	11	38%	.273
2018	OAK	MLB	27	3	1	0	55	0	62	55	13	2.8	9.1	63	25%	.256
2019	TBA	MLB	28	3	3	0	51	0	54	50	9	3.7	9.6	58	31%	.285

Breakout: 21%   Improve: 31%   Collapse: 26%   Attrition: 15%   MLB: 70%
Comparables: Pedro Baez, Matt Reynolds, Clay Zavada

The A's had a spare Ryon Healy sitting around and all his possible positions accounted for by better players (Matts Chapman and Olson on the infield corners and Khris Davis at DH), so they shipped him to Seattle for Pagan and teenage shortstop Alexander Campos in the 2018 offseason. Pagan had emerged the prior year as a middle-relief option with a mid-90s fastball that missed enough bats to overcome his extreme fly-ball ways. Bob Melvin was under no illusions about Pagan's upside, largely pitching him in low-leverage situations. As a four-seamer/slider hurler with only a show-me changeup, he has no weapons against lefties, and it showed in the .296/.376/.654 line he allowed to them. Given his ROOGY characteristics and the size of modern bullpens, his usage should probably be different going forward: 31 of his 89 career games have seen him pitch in multiple innings, but he's likely to see more success if he's kept away from all but the most harmless lefties.

YEAR	TEAM	LVL	AGE	WHIP	ERA	DRA	WARP	MPH	FB%	WHF	CSP
2016	WTN	AA	25	0.98	1.17	2.46	0.8				
2016	TAC	AAA	25	1.34	3.67	3.19	0.7				
2017	TAC	AAA	26	0.85	2.56	3.35	0.7				
2017	SEA	MLB	26	0.93	3.22	3.68	0.8	95.5	68.7	15	54.7
2018	NAS	AAA	27	0.83	3.00	1.33	0.3				
2018	OAK	MLB	27	1.19	4.35	4.35	0.4	95.7	66.4	15.5	50.9
2019	TBA	MLB	28	1.31	4.63	4.96	0.1	95.0	67.6	15.4	52.9

Tampa Bay Rays 2019

Emilio Pagan, continued

Pitch Shape vs LHH

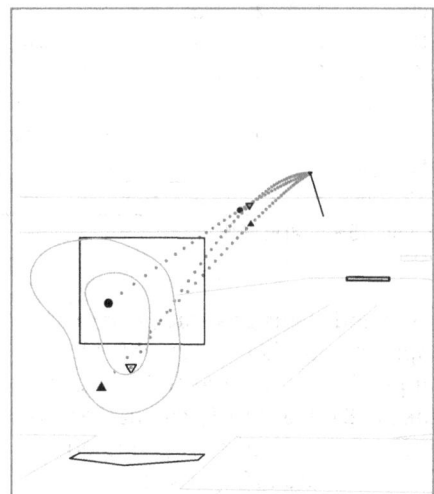

Pitch Shape vs RHH

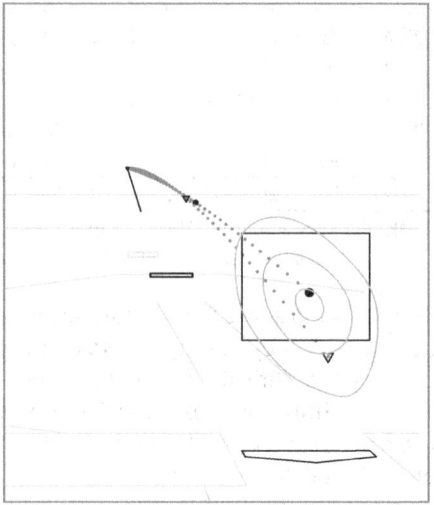

Type	Frequency	Velocity	H Movement	V Movement
● Fastball	65.2%	94.6 [107]	-3.2 [116]	-11.2 [114]
□ Sinker	1.2%	94.3 [109]	-11.6 [109]	-14.5 [119]
+ Cutter				
▲ Changeup	4.1%	87.8 [110]	-10.3 [105]	-21 [119]
× Splitter				
▽ Slider	29.5%	85.7 [105]	4.5 [99]	-32 [103]
◇ Curveball				
⊕ Slow Curveball				
✳ Knuckleball				
▼ Screwball				

Blake Snell LHP

Born: 12/04/92 Age: 26 Bats: L Throws: L
Height: 6'4" Weight: 200 Origin: Round 1, 2011 Draft (#52 overall)

YEAR	TEAM	LVL	AGE	W	L	SV	G	GS	IP	H	HR	BB/9	K/9	K	GB%	BABIP
2016	DUR	AAA	23	3	5	0	12	12	63	56	4	4.0	12.9	90	51%	.356
2016	TBA	MLB	23	6	8	0	19	19	89	93	5	5.2	9.9	98	39%	.356
2017	DUR	AAA	24	5	0	0	7	7	44	43	5	3.1	12.5	61	46%	.362
2017	TBA	MLB	24	5	7	0	24	24	129^1	113	15	4.1	8.3	119	45%	.278
2018	TBA	MLB	25	21	5	0	31	31	180^2	112	16	3.2	11.0	221	46%	.241
2019	TBA	MLB	26	11	8	0	29	29	165^1	133	15	3.8	10.6	194	44%	.292

Breakout: 31% Improve: 66% Collapse: 22% Attrition: 4% MLB: 93%
Comparables: Jon Gray, Matt Harvey, Brandon Beachy

Naturally, the team that bucked the trend of a traditional rotation ended up with the Cy Young-winning starting pitcher. Snell was basically one of the Rays' only two starters (first along with Chris Archer, and later Tyler Glasnow) for most of the season. He posted the lowest ERA (1.89) by an American League starter since 2000 and beat out Justin Verlander for the award despite fewer innings and somewhat lesser peripherals. Maturing in his mid-20s, Snell relied a little less on his fastball and increased the usage of his curveball while continuing to throw a changeup and slider. He struck out over 30 percent of the batters he faced and posted a career-high ground-ball rate. Of course, detractors will scream regression. Naturally, a sub-2.00 ERA is highly unsustainable, but Snell was a supplemental first-round pick (in a historically regrettable class for Tampa Bay), a top prospect and has the stuff to be an ace for years to come even with some slide.

YEAR	TEAM	LVL	AGE	WHIP	ERA	DRA	WARP	MPH	FB%	WHF	CSP
2016	DUR	AAA	23	1.33	3.29	2.57	2.0				
2016	TBA	MLB	23	1.62	3.54	5.25	0.1	96.2	57.2	11.8	43.5
2017	DUR	AAA	24	1.32	2.66	2.89	1.4				
2017	TBA	MLB	24	1.33	4.04	4.05	2.2	96.0	55.1	11.4	40.4
2018	TBA	MLB	25	0.97	1.89	2.44	6.0	97.7	51.5	15.7	44.5
2019	TBA	MLB	26	1.23	3.23	3.67	3.4	96.6	54.6	13.9	43.7

Blake Snell, continued

Pitch Shape vs LHH

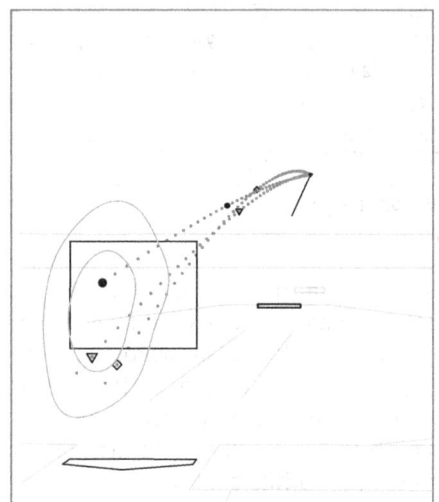

Pitch Shape vs RHH

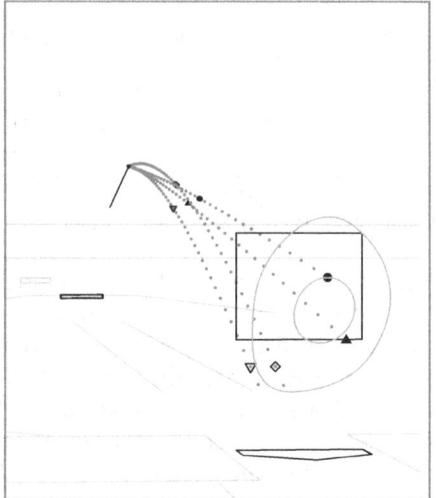

Type	Frequency	Velocity	H Movement	V Movement
● Fastball	51.5%	96.5 [113]	4.5 [110]	-10.5 [117]
☐ Sinker				
+ Cutter				
▲ Changeup	19.2%	88.1 [111]	12.2 [95]	-21.1 [119]
✕ Splitter				
▽ Slider	9.1%	88.7 [119]	-3.9 [96]	-28.9 [112]
◇ Curveball	20.2%	81.8 [112]	-4.8 [87]	-47.1 [102]
⊕ Slow Curveball				
✻ Knuckleball				
▼ Screwball				

Ryne Stanek RHP

Born: 07/26/91 Age: 27 Bats: R Throws: R
Height: 6'4" Weight: 215 Origin: Round 1, 2013 Draft (#29 overall)

YEAR	TEAM	LVL	AGE	W	L	SV	G	GS	IP	H	HR	BB/9	K/9	K	GB%	BABIP
2016	MNT	AA	24	2	6	2	18	11	78^1	64	6	4.0	10.5	91	53%	.307
2016	DUR	AAA	24	2	4	1	16	0	24^1	22	3	4.8	8.1	22	47%	.284
2017	DUR	AAA	25	3	0	8	37	0	44^2	26	0	3.2	12.1	60	40%	.268
2017	TBA	MLB	25	0	0	0	21	0	20	26	6	5.4	13.1	29	33%	.417
2018	DUR	AAA	26	0	1	2	10	0	9^2	5	1	5.6	15.8	17	59%	.250
2018	TBA	MLB	26	2	3	0	59	29	66^1	45	8	3.7	11.0	81	32%	.253
2019	TBA	MLB	27	4	5	0	48	16	65	54	8	4.2	10.8	79	40%	.291

Breakout: 19%   Improve: 39%   Collapse: 20%   Attrition: 27%   MLB: 72%
Comparables: Matt Barnes, Tom Mastny, Phil Coke

When he was selected with the 29th pick in the 2013 draft, experts were split on Stanek's ultimate role. Some saw the former Arkansas Razorback continuing his path as a starter, while others saw more viability as a reliever. They were both right, technically. Stanek was the first pitcher to throw a pitch for the Rays in 29 games. He started more games than James Paxton, Trevor Bauer and Chris Sale, to name a few. He also finished 10 games and tossed just 66 1/3 innings. Stanek was the Rays' choice du jour for most opening assignments, as his high-octane fastball married with a solid slider and split-finger made him a natural for the role. His shortcomings as a starter, endurance and control, were mitigated and his strengths highlighted. He held opponents below a .200 average regardless of when he entered the game and he never went through the order more than once. Obviously, the Rays would prefer five Blake Snells in the rotation, but there probably will be room for one Ryne Stanek in 2019 as they continue their most recent pitching strategy.

YEAR	TEAM	LVL	AGE	WHIP	ERA	DRA	WARP	MPH	FB%	WHF	CSP
2016	MNT	AA	24	1.26	3.79	3.28	1.6				
2016	DUR	AAA	24	1.44	5.92	3.71	0.3				
2017	DUR	AAA	25	0.94	1.21	3.10	1.1				
2017	TBA	MLB	25	1.90	5.85	2.67	0.6	100.0	67.1	16.3	44.4
2018	DUR	AAA	26	1.14	1.86	1.10	0.4				
2018	TBA	MLB	26	1.09	2.98	3.34	1.4	99.4	60.1	16.9	44.1
2019	TBA	MLB	27	1.29	3.66	4.14	0.9	99.0	62.5	17	44.8

Ryne Stanek, continued

Pitch Shape vs LHH
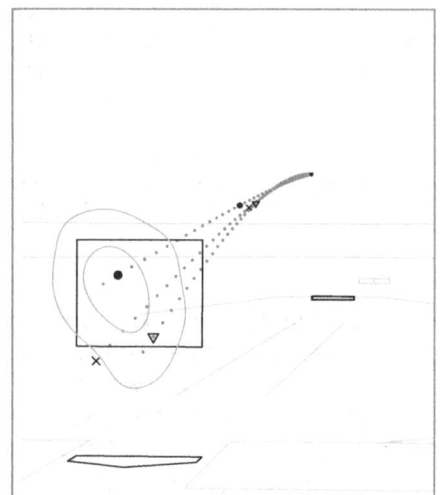

Pitch Shape vs RHH
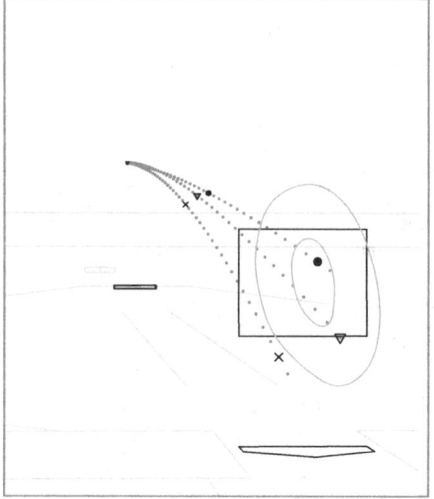

Type	Frequency	Velocity	H Movement	V Movement
● Fastball	60.1%	98.4 [119]	-6.6 [100]	-9.8 [119]
☐ Sinker				
+ Cutter				
▲ Changeup				
✕ Splitter	13.6%	88.6 [116]	-8 [101]	-28 [106]
▽ Slider	26.3%	89.5 [123]	1.8 [87]	-28.4 [114]
◇ Curveball				
⊕ Slow Curveball				
✱ Knuckleball				
▼ Screwball				

Hunter Wood   RHP

Born: 08/12/93   Age: 25   Bats: R   Throws: R
Height: 6'1"   Weight: 165   Origin: Round 29, 2013 Draft (#878 overall)

YEAR	TEAM	LVL	AGE	W	L	SV	G	GS	IP	H	HR	BB/9	K/9	K	GB%	BABIP
2016	PCH	A+	22	3	3	0	11	9	63^2	34	2	3.4	7.9	56	48%	.194
2016	MNT	AA	22	6	2	0	10	9	49^1	36	5	3.6	8.9	49	25%	.250
2017	TBA	MLB	23	0	0	0	1	0	0^1	0	0	0.0	0.0	0	0%	.000
2017	MNT	AA	23	4	4	0	12	12	70	68	7	3.1	8.7	68	38%	.319
2017	DUR	AAA	23	3	1	0	19	6	53^1	54	8	3.4	7.9	47	46%	.299
2018	DUR	AAA	24	2	2	3	24	2	42	26	4	2.1	13.5	63	46%	.262
2018	TBA	MLB	24	1	1	0	29	8	41	42	4	4.0	9.2	42	44%	.330
2019	TBA	MLB	25	3	2	0	51	0	54	43	5	3.8	10.3	62	40%	.282

Breakout: 11%   Improve: 43%   Collapse: 22%   Attrition: 26%   MLB: 76%
Comparables: Steven Matz, Nick Tropeano, Jose Capellan

Wood was another hybrid for Tampa Bay, but unlike for most, it's a role he's held for a little bit. Wood split his 140 minor-league appearances almost evenly, with 73 starts and 67 as a reliever. He pitches mainly off a mid-90s fastball, with a cutter coming in just a few notches slower. He can also throw a changeup and mixes in a slow curveball. The hook was very useful, holding batters to a .179 average, and it was the put-away offering on 35 percent of his strikeouts. At some point there will be a numbers crunch as some of the Rays' younger arms mature and get healthy. Wood would be on the bubble, but he has the skill set to be useful even in a regular relief sense.

YEAR	TEAM	LVL	AGE	WHIP	ERA	DRA	WARP	MPH	FB%	WHF	CSP
2016	PCH	A+	22	0.91	1.70	3.96	1.1				
2016	MNT	AA	22	1.14	3.28	3.27	1.1				
2017	TBA	MLB	23	0.00	0.00	4.12	0.0	89.7	40	0	38.2
2017	MNT	AA	23	1.31	4.76	3.61	1.3				
2017	DUR	AAA	23	1.39	4.39	4.12	0.8				
2018	DUR	AAA	24	0.86	3.00	2.26	1.4				
2018	TBA	MLB	24	1.46	3.73	2.97	1.0	96.1	52.7	14.4	45.6
2019	TBA	MLB	25	1.20	3.29	3.85	0.8	95.8	53.9	14.6	43.4

Tampa Bay Rays 2019

Hunter Wood, continued

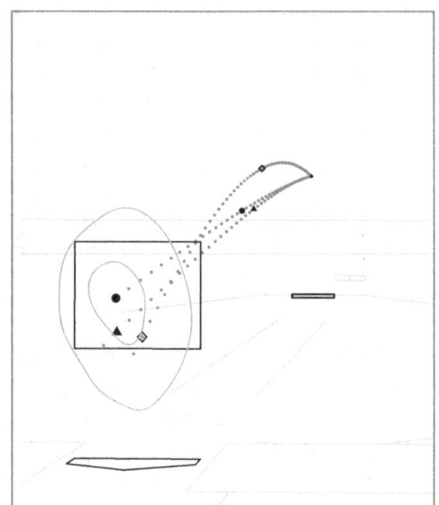
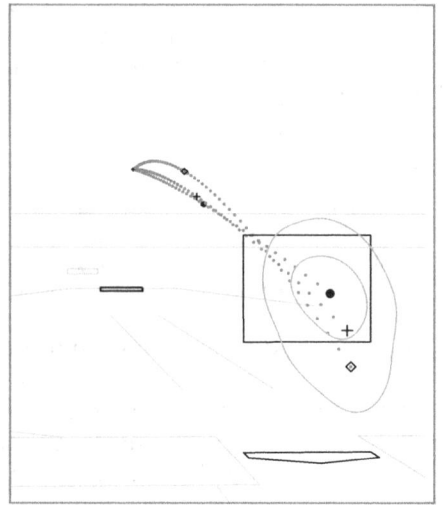

Type	Frequency	Velocity	H Movement	V Movement
● Fastball	52.7%	94.9 [108]	-0.9 [127]	-10.1 [118]
☐ Sinker				
+ Cutter	22.4%	87.9 [95]	5.5 [121]	-26.6 [88]
▲ Changeup	6.9%	86.9 [106]	-8 [117]	-20.4 [121]
× Splitter				
▽ Slider				
◇ Curveball	18.0%	76 [91]	5.2 [89]	-58.8 [76]
⊕ Slow Curveball				
✳ Knuckleball				
▼ Screwball				

Ryan Yarbrough LHP

Born: 12/31/91 Age: 27 Bats: R Throws: L
Height: 6'5" Weight: 205 Origin: Round 4, 2014 Draft (#111 overall)

YEAR	TEAM	LVL	AGE	W	L	SV	G	GS	IP	H	HR	BB/9	K/9	K	GB%	BABIP
2016	WTN	AA	24	12	4	0	25	25	128^1	112	7	2.2	6.9	99	50%	.276
2017	DUR	AAA	25	13	6	0	26	26	157^1	144	20	2.2	9.1	159	47%	.296
2018	TBA	MLB	26	16	6	0	38	6	147^1	140	18	3.1	7.8	128	39%	.288
2019	TBA	MLB	27	6	7	0	93	10	118	112	17	3.2	8.3	108	43%	.287

Breakout: 28% Improve: 50% Collapse: 16% Attrition: 24% MLB: 84%
Comparables: Jacob deGrom, Joe Saunders, Brandon Workman

The Rays' appointed bulk guy, Yarbrough was a starter for the majority of his career prior to 2018. He started just six times in his rookie season, yet recorded 16 wins and tossed nearly 150 innings as the follower to the Rays' opener strategy. One day, he'll be a fascinating arbitration case, combining the workload of a fifth starter with the appearances of a middle reliever. Of his 32 relief appearances, 11 of them lasted at least five innings, including one seven-inning effort. The poster boy for why the Rays employ such a strategy, the lefty posted a 3.31 FIP the first time though the order and a 5.36 FIP in the rare instances he flipped a lineup twice. Despite being 6-foot-5, he's a finesse lefty with an average heater below 90 mph. He uses a cutter with similar velocity almost as much as the straight fastball, and spins a slider and changeup to balance things out. The tandem (or law firm) of Stanek and Yarbrough represent the ideal pairing for the Rays' strategy. They are opposite in hand and stuff, with some warts in full-time roles, but mixed together you get almost the same first name and 200 pretty good innings.

YEAR	TEAM	LVL	AGE	WHIP	ERA	DRA	WARP	MPH	FB%	WHF	CSP
2016	WTN	AA	24	1.11	2.95	3.25	2.8				
2017	DUR	AAA	25	1.16	3.43	3.41	4.0				
2018	TBA	MLB	26	1.29	3.91	4.82	0.3	91.1	63.9	10	50.6
2019	TBA	MLB	27	1.30	4.36	4.79	0.6	90.6	64.6	10.1	51.2

Ryan Yarbrough, continued

Pitch Shape vs LHH

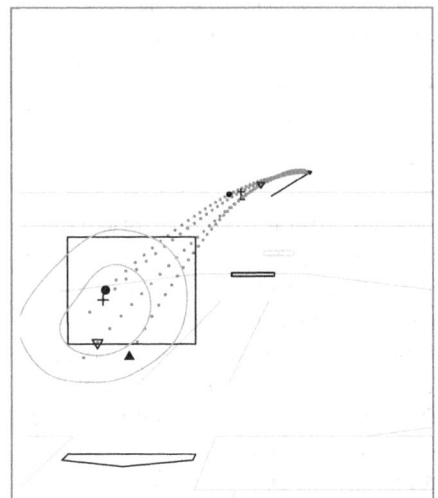

Pitch Shape vs RHH

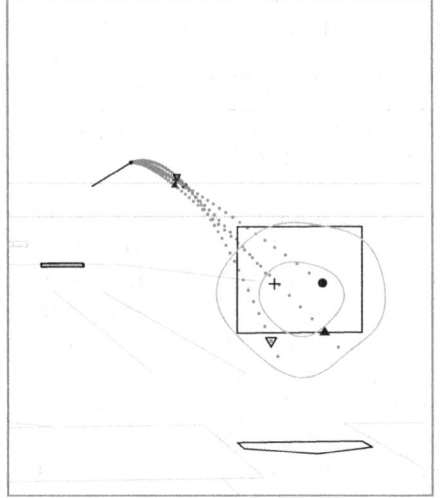

Type	Frequency	Velocity	H Movement	V Movement
● Fastball	32.5%	89.9 [92]	12.7 [72]	-19.2 [89]
☐ Sinker				
+ Cutter	31.3%	87.5 [93]	1.5 [80]	-24 [99]
▲ Changeup	25.0%	81.9 [86]	16.2 [74]	-31.7 [87]
✕ Splitter				
▽ Slider	11.0%	77.1 [67]	-9.6 [120]	-39.1 [82]
◇ Curveball	0.2%	78.7 [101]	-7.6 [99]	-37.1 [125]
⊕ Slow Curveball				
✳ Knuckleball				
▼ Screwball				

Vidal Brujan 2B

Born: 02/09/98 Age: 21 Bats: B Throws: R
Height: 5'9" Weight: 155 Origin: International Free Agent, 2014

YEAR	TEAM	LVL	AGE	PA	R	2B	3B	HR	RBI	BB	K	SB	CS	AVG/OBP/SLG
2016	RAY	RK	18	223	41	12	5	1	8	14	15	8	5	.282/.344/.406
2017	HUD	A-	19	302	51	15	5	3	20	34	36	16	8	.285/.378/.415
2018	BGR	A	20	434	86	18	5	5	41	48	53	43	15	.313/.395/.427
2018	PCH	A+	20	114	26	7	2	4	12	15	15	12	4	.347/.434/.582
2019	TBA	MLB	21	251	29	7	1	6	19	12	50	9	3	.180/.220/.293

Breakout: 23% Improve: 31% Collapse: 1% Attrition: 13% MLB: 32%
Comparables: Mookie Betts, Jose Ramirez, Jonathan Schoop

Scouting types thought Brujan had a breakout in 2017. They were a year off, because 2018 was a true arrival. Playing for Bowling Green and later Charlotte, he hit .320 on the season, reached base 40 percent of the time and tallied extra bases 41 times. He also stole an astounding 55 bags even though he was caught 19 times. Signed for less than a waiver claim in 2014, he has leadoff ability with excellent contact skills and exceptional speed. His arm is average-ish, which is why he plays right of the bag up the middle. Brujan is a level or two behind the logjam at the keystone for Tampa Bay. However, at this accelerated pace, he may get there much sooner than expected.

YEAR	TEAM	LVL	AGE	PA	DRC+	VORP	BABIP	BRR	FRAA	WARP
2016	RAY	RK	18	223	140	14.9	.301	1.8	2B(49): 3.8	1.2
2017	HUD	A-	19	302	148	20.6	.321	-3.7	2B(65): 14.9	2.6
2018	BGR	A	20	434	141	41.0	.351	8.2	2B(88): 4.4	4.0
2018	PCH	A+	20	114	165	13.9	.380	1.0	2B(24): 4.5	1.4
2019	TBA	MLB	21	251	37	-9.4	.201	1.1	2B 5	-0.5

Nick Ciuffo C

Born: 03/07/95 Age: 24 Bats: L Throws: R
Height: 6'1" Weight: 205 Origin: Round 1, 2013 Draft (#21 overall)

YEAR	TEAM	LVL	AGE	PA	R	2B	3B	HR	RBI	BB	K	SB	CS	AVG/OBP/SLG
2016	PCH	A+	21	242	16	8	0	0	15	9	45	2	3	.262/.288/.297
2017	MNT	AA	22	417	42	29	1	7	42	42	95	2	0	.245/.319/.385
2018	DUR	AAA	23	236	26	11	0	5	28	13	62	0	0	.262/.301/.380
2018	TBA	MLB	23	44	3	1	0	1	5	3	12	0	0	.189/.262/.297
2019	TBA	MLB	24	75	8	4	0	2	7	5	21	0	0	.232/.280/.377

Breakout: 15% Improve: 27% Collapse: 0% Attrition: 24% MLB: 37%
Comparables: Jeff Mathis, Tony Cruz, Luis Exposito

A former 2013 first-round pick, Ciuffo finally made his MLB debut in 2018, but not before some dramatics. Left off the 40-man roster last winter, Ciuffo was subjected to testing for drugs of abuse. He failed for the second time and was forced to miss the first 50 games. He returned to mixed results. His offense remains behind his defense, but his defense is major-league caliber on its own. When the Rays selected veteran Adam Moore to be the third catcher it looked like Ciuffo's season would end in the minors. Moore, however, did not have his passport in order and could not join the club in Toronto. Ciuffo was able to enter Canada and took most of the reps behind the plate for the month of September. The lefty batter has considerable pull-side pop, but does not make much contact otherwise. Even if he never hits for much, his ability behind the plate will keep him employed. He has plus receiving skills with the arm to change the running game. He's a bit like Mike Zunino from the left side with lesser power.

YEAR	TEAM	P. COUNT	FRM RUNS	BLK RUNS	THRW RUNS	TOT RUNS
2017	MNT	10149	-11.8	-3.1	0.1	-13.5
2018	DUR	7350	5.2	0.0	1.2	6.4
2018	TBA	1790	-0.4	-0.6	0.0	-0.2
2019	TBA	2799	-1.6	-0.8	0.2	-2.2

YEAR	TEAM	LVL	AGE	PA	DRC+	VORP	BABIP	BRR	FRAA	WARP
2016	PCH	A+	21	242	74	-4.9	.323	-3.0	C(50): 2.9	-0.1
2017	MNT	AA	22	417	104	14.7	.308	-1.6	C(70): -14.7	-0.9
2018	DUR	AAA	23	236	91	4.5	.340	-2.8	C(55): 5.6	0.8
2018	TBA	MLB	23	44	75	0.0	.240	-0.1	C(16): -1.2	-0.1
2019	TBA	MLB	24	75	66	0.3	.296	-0.1	C -3	-0.3

Wander Franco SS

Born: 03/01/01   Age: 18   Bats: B   Throws: R
Height: 5'10"   Weight: 189   Origin: International Free Agent, 2017

YEAR	TEAM	LVL	AGE	PA	R	2B	3B	HR	RBI	BB	K	SB	CS	AVG/OBP/SLG
2018	PRI	RK	17	273	46	10	7	11	57	27	19	4	3	.351/.418/.587
2019	TBA	MLB	18	251	22	4	2	9	29	7	50	0	0	.196/.217/.339

Comparables: Adalberto Mondesi, Wilmer Flores, Tommy Brown

If you don't know, now you know. Franco will be one of the most talked about prospects of 2019 after putting up insane numbers in his first pro season. Not bad for someone who won't legally be an adult until March. The Rays' farm system is filled with a lot of quality prospects, but there's not much star projection. Not only does Franco have that, you can add *super* in front of it. That's why the club paid nearly $4 million to sign him in 2017. He has at least four above-average-or-better tools and is a shortstop until he's not. He has exceptional bat speed, strong hands, and can run and throw really well. The nephew of Willy and Erick Aybar could be the top overall prospect in MLB by the 2020 edition of this book.

YEAR	TEAM	LVL	AGE	PA	DRC+	VORP	BABIP	BRR	FRAA	WARP
2018	PRI	RK	17	273	179	35.3	.346	-0.4	SS(53): -5.3	1.6
2019	TBA	MLB	18	251	46	-6.8	.206	0.1	SS -2	-0.9

Ronaldo Hernandez C
Born: 11/11/97   Age: 21   Bats: R   Throws: R
Height: 6'1"   Weight: 185   Origin: International Free Agent, 2014

YEAR	TEAM	LVL	AGE	PA	R	2B	3B	HR	RBI	BB	K	SB	CS	AVG/OBP/SLG
2016	DDR	RK	18	229	34	12	0	6	35	20	12	3	5	.340/.406/.485
2017	PRI	RK	19	246	42	22	1	5	40	16	39	2	2	.332/.382/.507
2018	BGR	A	20	449	68	20	1	21	79	31	69	10	4	.284/.339/.494
2019	TBA	MLB	21	251	22	10	0	9	29	4	59	1	0	.204/.214/.353

Breakout: 16%   Improve: 24%   Collapse: 1%   Attrition: 19%   MLB: 28%
Comparables: Francisco Mejia, Austin Romine, Gary Sanchez

Developing catchers has been an organizational struggle for Tampa Bay since its inception. Miguel Perez, Nick Ciuffo and Mike Zunino give them youth and potential at the position now, but Hernandez could be the one they've been waiting for. The Rays made him a backstop after signing him out of Colombia in 2014, part of the same J2 class as Jesus Sanchez. He followed an impressive 2017 in the Appalachian League with a strong showing in the Midwest League, finishing second in home runs (21) and third in slugging percentage. Defensively, he continues to grow, with most feeling he'll be able to handle the gig as he progresses with the arm to control the running game. Despite being a converted infielder, he runs like a natural catcher.

YEAR	TEAM	LVL	AGE	PA	DRC+	VORP	BABIP	BRR	FRAA	WARP
2016	DDR	RK	18	229	175	28.8	.340	-1.2	C(27): -0.3, C(5): -0.3	1.9
2017	PRI	RK	19	246	160	23.7	.379	2.5	C(43): 1.1	1.9
2018	BGR	A	20	449	132	39.2	.292	-0.8	C(85): 1.2	2.8
2019	TBA	MLB	21	251	47	-5.6	.228	-0.4	C 0	-0.6

Joshua Lowe OF

Born: 02/02/98 Age: 21 Bats: L Throws: R
Height: 6'4" Weight: 205 Origin: Round 1, 2016 Draft (#13 overall)

YEAR	TEAM	LVL	AGE	PA	R	2B	3B	HR	RBI	BB	K	SB	CS	AVG/OBP/SLG
2016	RAY	RK	18	114	14	6	1	2	15	20	27	1	1	.258/.386/.409
2016	PRI	RK	18	100	11	0	2	3	11	17	32	1	1	.238/.360/.400
2017	BGR	A	19	507	60	26	2	8	55	42	144	22	8	.268/.326/.386
2018	PCH	A+	20	455	62	25	3	6	47	47	117	18	6	.238/.322/.361
2019	TBA	MLB	21	251	25	5	0	6	19	16	89	4	1	.150/.202/.252

Breakout: 1%   Improve: 5%   Collapse: 0%   Attrition: 2%   MLB: 5%
Comparables: Michael Saunders, Daniel Fields, Joe Benson

Lowe got the bragging rights of being a first-round pick over brother Nate, who was selected in the 13th round in 2016. But the younger bro has some catching up to do in terms of development. After dominating the lowest levels of the system, he struggled in the Florida State League in 2018. He struck out 26 percent of the time—actually an improvement from 2017's 28 percent—and did not make enough hard contact in the thick South Florida air to overlook that number despite owning plus raw power. He has good speed and remained in center field after converting from third base in 2017. Lowe will likely start the season as a 21-year-old in Double-A, which means there's plenty of time to catch and pass big brother.

YEAR	TEAM	LVL	AGE	PA	DRC+	VORP	BABIP	BRR	FRAA	WARP
2016	RAY	RK	18	114	158	10.1	.338	0.9	3B(22): 0.8	0.7
2016	PRI	RK	18	100	117	6.0	.333	0.4	3B(23): -3.4	-0.2
2017	BGR	A	19	507	101	21.8	.369	2.3	CF(112): 3.4	1.5
2018	PCH	A+	20	455	95	14.8	.318	1.1	CF(102): 4.1	0.8
2019	TBA	MLB	21	251	17	-15.3	.204	0.1	CF 1	-1.5

Nathaniel Lowe 1B

Born: 07/07/95   Age: 23   Bats: L   Throws: R
Height: 6'4"   Weight: 235   Origin: Round 13, 2016 Draft (#390 overall)

YEAR	TEAM	LVL	AGE	PA	R	2B	3B	HR	RBI	BB	K	SB	CS	AVG/OBP/SLG
2016	HUD	A-	20	285	26	18	2	4	40	30	39	1	0	.300/.382/.437
2017	BGR	A	21	269	34	13	0	5	35	36	53	0	1	.293/.387/.415
2017	PCH	A+	21	203	21	10	1	2	24	28	53	1	1	.249/.355/.353
2018	PCH	A+	22	220	39	15	0	10	44	25	33	0	0	.356/.432/.588
2018	MNT	AA	22	225	36	11	0	13	42	35	30	1	1	.340/.444/.606
2018	DUR	AAA	22	110	18	6	1	4	16	8	27	0	0	.260/.327/.460
2019	TBA	MLB	23	239	30	10	1	9	27	22	55	0	0	.237/.308/.419

Breakout: 10%   Improve: 29%   Collapse: 5%   Attrition: 23%   MLB: 47%
Comparables: Ji-Man Choi, Rhys Hoskins, Travis Shaw

The older brother of Josh, selected 12 rounds later in the same draft, Nate is on pace to beat little bro to the big leagues after a laser show in 2018. Starting the season in Charlotte, he ended it on the major's door in Durham. He collected 27 home runs and 32 doubles along the way while hitting for average and taking walks, too. Typically the hulking left-handed hitter would be projected as a platoon bat. That may ultimately be the case, but he has more than held his own against southpaws thus far. Lowe is certainly a fast riser, but even at this accelerated pace, there are left-handed-hitting first basemen ahead of him on the depth chart. Working in Lowe's favor is that neither of them can match his power potential.

YEAR	TEAM	LVL	AGE	PA	DRC+	VORP	BABIP	BRR	FRAA	WARP
2016	HUD	A-	20	285	165	20.7	.338	1.2	1B(65): 2.9	1.8
2017	BGR	A	21	269	136	14.0	.356	-0.2	1B(49): 0.2	1.0
2017	PCH	A+	21	203	108	0.6	.345	-0.5	1B(51): -1.5	-0.3
2018	PCH	A+	22	220	207	22.6	.391	-2.4	1B(35): -2.9	1.7
2018	MNT	AA	22	225	211	33.7	.349	1.9	1B(39): -0.4	2.7
2018	DUR	AAA	22	110	116	1.4	.319	-1.2	1B(25): -0.1	0.0
2019	TBA	MLB	23	239	89	0.7	.270	-0.4	1B -1	0.0

Brendan McKay 1B

Born: 12/18/95 Age: 23 Bats: L Throws: L
Height: 6'2" Weight: 212 Origin: Round 1, 2017 Draft (#4 overall)

YEAR	TEAM	LVL	AGE	PA	R	2B	3B	HR	RBI	BB	K	SB	CS	AVG/OBP/SLG
2017	HUD	A-	21	149	16	4	1	4	22	21	33	2	0	.232/.349/.376
2018	BGR	A	22	91	12	2	0	1	16	28	13	0	0	.254/.484/.333
2018	PCH	A+	22	139	19	6	1	5	21	16	38	0	0	.210/.317/.403
2019	TBA	MLB	23	251	22	4	0	8	26	25	74	0	0	.141/.228/.268

Breakout: 6%   Improve: 17%   Collapse: 0%   Attrition: 16%   MLB: 21%
Comparables: Chris Parmelee, Chris McGuiness, Max Muncy

The first legitimate two-way player drafted in decades, McKay watched Shohei Otani put the blueprint together for a player to hit and pitch for a major-league team. McKay was a top-five pick and played at a major university, but the Rays have brought him along relatively slowly considering his age and experience. A few non-threatening injuries have also slowed the process. As it stands, the former Louisville Cardinal is much farther down the line as a pitcher than he is as a hitter, where he's yet to display that 20-homer potential he was projected to have. On the other hand, McKay the pitcher has been dominant. The organization was already cautious in his usage, but that was not enough to prevent multiple oblique injuries that cost him development. Although his pitching is way ahead of his hitting, the Rays will let him play both ways until it looks like he cannot.

YEAR	TEAM	LVL	AGE	PA	DRC+	VORP	BABIP	BRR	FRAA	WARP
2017	HUD	A-	21	149	117	3.8	.281	-1.3	1B(21): -1.1, P(6): 0.1	-0.2
2018	BGR	A	22	91	175	1.0	.306	-3.1	1B(9): -0.3, P(6): 0.1	0.4
2018	PCH	A+	22	139	96	1.6	.260	0.5	1B(18): -0.4, P(11): -0.3	-0.2
2019	TBA	MLB	23	251	34	-15.9	.163	-0.4	1B -2	-1.9

Jesus Sanchez RF

Born: 10/07/97   Age: 21   Bats: L   Throws: R
Height: 6'3"   Weight: 210   Origin: International Free Agent, 2014

YEAR	TEAM	LVL	AGE	PA	R	2B	3B	HR	RBI	BB	K	SB	CS	AVG/OBP/SLG
2016	RAY	RK	18	173	25	6	8	4	31	6	31	1	5	.323/.341/.530
2016	PRI	RK	18	53	8	4	0	3	8	3	12	1	0	.347/.385/.612
2017	BGR	A	19	512	81	29	4	15	82	32	91	7	2	.305/.348/.478
2018	PCH	A+	20	378	56	24	2	10	64	15	71	6	3	.301/.331/.462
2018	MNT	AA	20	110	14	8	0	1	11	11	21	1	1	.214/.300/.327
2019	TBA	MLB	21	251	21	10	0	8	28	7	67	1	0	.200/.219/.339

Breakout: 5%   Improve: 15%   Collapse: 0%   Attrition: 9%   MLB: 16%
Comparables: Justin Williams, Jorge Bonifacio, Marcell Ozuna

On the heels of a strong 2017 showing, his first year with a full-season affiliate, Sanchez had considerable hype heading into 2018. It came in waves, but he was very good during the humid summer in Port Charlotte. He showed solid pop despite hitting in thick air and did not have to sell out for that with strikeouts. Sanchez is not one for walks and that will have to change at some point, as he does not have the 80-grade bat to make up for the on-base opportunities. He did take a few more free passes upon promotion to Double-A, but otherwise struggled in Montgomery, although reaching the Southern League as a 20-year-old is a feat unto itself. He's long, with average speed and the arm to handle right field. He's at least a year away, but should be arriving in the middle of the Rays' opening window.

YEAR	TEAM	LVL	AGE	PA	DRC+	VORP	BABIP	BRR	FRAA	WARP
2016	RAY	RK	18	173	145	13.7	.371	-0.9	CF(31): 1.9, RF(10): -1.3	0.6
2016	PRI	RK	18	53	175	7.5	.412	0.9	LF(11): 0.5, CF(3): -0.1	0.4
2017	BGR	A	19	512	127	29.4	.349	3.4	LF(78): 14.0, RF(19): -0.5	3.6
2018	PCH	A+	20	378	133	20.0	.350	-1.5	RF(78): 1.8, CF(7): -1.4	1.2
2018	MNT	AA	20	110	93	-0.8	.263	0.7	RF(26): -0.8, CF(1): 0.0	-0.1
2019	TBA	MLB	21	251	44	-10.3	.238	-0.5	RF -1, CF 0	-1.2

Nick Solak UT

Born: 01/11/95 Age: 24 Bats: R Throws: R
Height: 5'11" Weight: 175 Origin: Round 2, 2016 Draft (#62 overall)

YEAR	TEAM	LVL	AGE	PA	R	2B	3B	HR	RBI	BB	K	SB	CS	AVG/OBP/SLG
2016	STA	A-	21	279	48	13	1	3	25	30	39	8	0	.321/.412/.421
2017	TAM	A+	22	406	56	17	4	10	44	53	76	13	4	.301/.397/.460
2017	TRN	AA	22	132	16	9	1	2	9	10	24	1	1	.286/.344/.429
2018	MNT	AA	23	565	91	17	3	19	76	68	112	21	6	.282/.384/.450
2019	TBA	MLB	24	251	28	7	1	8	29	19	61	4	1	.226/.296/.368

Breakout: 12% Improve: 33% Collapse: 5% Attrition: 27% MLB: 61%
Comparables: Rob Refsnyder, Devon Travis, Jason Kipnis

A second-round pick in 2016, Solak landed with the Rays in a three-team deal with the Yankees and Diamondbacks. Once projected as a speedy slap hitter, he's developed some pop. After hitting 12 home runs in 2017, he belted 19 to place fourth in the Southern League. He also finished fourth in batting average and paced the league in on-base percentage while stealing 21 bags. After playing second base exclusively with the Yankees, he branched out into left and center field as well. The Rays have at least a half-dozen viable players with a variety of offensive skill sets at second base. It will be a *Hunger Games*-style battle to see who wins, with the odds being somewhat in Solak's favor.

YEAR	TEAM	LVL	AGE	PA	DRC+	VORP	BABIP	BRR	FRAA	WARP
2016	STA	A-	21	279	171	25.0	.372	3.6	2B(59): -1.9	2.1
2017	TAM	A+	22	406	161	38.8	.357	2.5	2B(92): 1.4	3.1
2017	TRN	AA	22	132	105	8.3	.340	0.5	2B(30): 2.0	0.5
2018	MNT	AA	23	565	138	46.4	.330	-0.5	2B(61): -6.9, LF(40): -3.3	1.7
2019	TBA	MLB	24	251	81	2.9	.273	0.2	2B 0, LF -1	0.2

Andrew Velazquez UT

Born: 07/14/94 Age: 24 Bats: B Throws: R
Height: 5'10" Weight: 160 Origin: Round 7, 2012 Draft (#243 overall)

YEAR	TEAM	LVL	AGE	PA	R	2B	3B	HR	RBI	BB	K	SB	CS	AVG/OBP/SLG
2016	PCH	A+	21	313	31	6	2	1	14	21	71	11	6	.262/.313/.308
2017	MNT	AA	22	414	49	17	4	9	37	30	112	18	9	.235/.297/.374
2018	MNT	AA	23	36	5	2	1	2	4	1	11	2	0	.229/.250/.514
2018	DUR	AAA	23	461	63	16	6	12	41	34	124	29	3	.258/.317/.409
2018	TBA	MLB	23	12	3	1	0	0	0	1	3	1	0	.300/.417/.400
2019	TBA	MLB	24	58	7	2	0	2	6	3	18	2	1	.222/.263/.370

Breakout: 14%   Improve: 21%   Collapse: 0%   Attrition: 17%   MLB: 24%
Comparables: Pat Valaika, Orlando Calixte, Grant Green

The dark horse on the depth chart, Velazquez has taken longer to develop because of nagging injuries and ineffectiveness. Acquired in a 2014 trade for Jeremy Hellickson, he finally broke through and became a major leaguer for the first time in 2018. He has much more pop than you'd expect from someone listed at 160 pounds. Once a projected starter, Velazquez should settle as a useful reserve with the ability to play all over the diamond and switch-hit. In just 13 games with the big-league club, he appeared at six different positions. There are more well-known names with better pedigrees, but the Bronx, New York native should provide a lot of value @for_dah_money he will make.

YEAR	TEAM	LVL	AGE	PA	DRC+	VORP	BABIP	BRR	FRAA	WARP
2016	PCH	A+	21	313	85	5.9	.343	1.6	SS(51): -3.4, 3B(11): -0.9	-0.3
2017	MNT	AA	22	414	79	8.7	.312	2.5	SS(82): 3.5, CF(16): 1.6	0.7
2018	MNT	AA	23	36	80	2.2	.273	0.8	CF(7): 1.6	0.2
2018	DUR	AAA	23	461	96	22.3	.338	5.8	SS(69): -1.8, CF(33): 3.5	1.7
2018	TBA	MLB	23	12	89	1.5	.429	0.5	3B(4): 0.0, CF(2): -0.2	0.1
2019	TBA	MLB	24	58	65	-0.1	.278	0.4	CF 0, RF 0	0.0

Shane Baz RHP

Born: 06/17/99 Age: 20 Bats: R Throws: R
Height: 6'3" Weight: 190 Origin: Round 1, 2017 Draft (#12 overall)

YEAR	TEAM	LVL	AGE	W	L	SV	G	GS	IP	H	HR	BB/9	K/9	K	GB%	BABIP
2017	PIR	RK	18	0	3	0	10	10	23^2	26	2	5.3	7.2	19	51%	.348
2018	BRI	RK	19	4	3	0	10	10	45^1	45	2	4.6	10.7	54	64%	.344
2018	PRI	RK	19	0	2	0	2	2	7	11	1	7.7	6.4	5	48%	.417
2019	TBA	MLB	20	2	4	0	10	10	37^2	39	5	8.6	6.7	28	52%	.298

Comparables: Sandy Alcantara, Wandy Peralta, Clay Holmes

When the Rays traded Chris Archer to the Pirates, they received two young, talented major leaguers in Austin Meadows and Tyler Glasnow. That would have been a pretty good haul. They also received a player to be named who turned out to be Baz, the 12th overall pick in the 2017 draft. He has the potential for three or four plus offerings, with a frame that's athletic and room to add some bulk. Baz has yet to make his full-season debut and control has been a concern in both reports and in games, so the range of outcomes is large. If Shane is as Baz as he wants to be he can have a front-of-the-rotation ceiling and a back-of-the-bullpen downside.

YEAR	TEAM	LVL	AGE	WHIP	ERA	DRA	WARP	MPH	FB%	WHF	CSP
2017	PIR	RK	18	1.69	3.80	5.57	0.1				
2018	BRI	RK	19	1.50	3.97	4.64	0.7				
2018	PRI	RK	19	2.43	7.71	10.04	-0.3				
2019	TBA	MLB	20	2.00	6.50	7.06	-0.7				

Ian Gibaut RHP

Born: 11/19/93 Age: 25 Bats: R Throws: R
Height: 6'3" Weight: 250 Origin: Round 11, 2015 Draft (#328 overall)

YEAR	TEAM	LVL	AGE	W	L	SV	G	GS	IP	H	HR	BB/9	K/9	K	GB%	BABIP
2016	BGR	A	22	1	0	1	7	0	9^2	6	0	0.9	16.8	18	33%	.333
2016	PCH	A+	22	1	2	3	27	0	47^1	45	2	3.6	8.6	45	37%	.326
2017	PCH	A+	23	1	0	2	5	0	8^1	5	0	1.1	15.1	14	33%	.333
2017	MNT	AA	23	6	1	10	43	0	52^2	33	6	4.4	10.8	63	44%	.221
2018	DUR	AAA	24	4	3	14	48	0	56	35	3	3.4	12.1	75	49%	.269
2019	TBA	MLB	25	1	1	0	19	0	20^1	16	2	4.4	10.7	24	42%	.291

Breakout: 8% Improve: 10% Collapse: 17% Attrition: 23% MLB: 31%
Comparables: Justin Miller, Cory Gearrin, Jacob Rhame

Sorry Corliss Williamson, Gibaut is the new "Big Nasty." The Tulane product is as conventional as they come for a reliever. He throws a hard fastball and backs that with a dirty slide piece. He also tosses a changeup that's more than just a show-me offering and can get left-handed hitters out. The burly right-hander has posted strikeout numbers to match his size since turning pro and improved his control with a promotion to Triple-A, after which he was added to the 40-man roster this winter. The word open, opener or some variation will be said a nauseating amount of times in this chapter. However, Big Nasty's future role is somewhat of a dirty word around these parts. He has "closer" stuff and potential.

YEAR	TEAM	LVL	AGE	WHIP	ERA	DRA	WARP	MPH	FB%	WHF	CSP
2016	BGR	A	22	0.72	0.93	0.10	0.5				
2016	PCH	A+	22	1.35	2.85	3.15	1.0				
2017	PCH	A+	23	0.72	2.16	2.80	0.2				
2017	MNT	AA	23	1.12	2.22	3.12	1.1				
2018	DUR	AAA	24	1.00	2.09	3.00	1.4				
2019	TBA	MLB	25	1.29	3.56	4.07	0.3				

Brent Honeywell   RHP

Born: 03/31/95   Age: 24   Bats: R   Throws: R
Height: 6'2"   Weight: 180   Origin: Round 2, 2014 Draft (#72 overall)

YEAR	TEAM	LVL	AGE	W	L	SV	G	GS	IP	H	HR	BB/9	K/9	K	GB%	BABIP
2016	PCH	A+	21	4	1	0	10	10	56	43	5	1.8	10.3	64	33%	.279
2016	MNT	AA	21	3	2	0	10	10	59^1	51	4	2.1	8.0	53	29%	.287
2017	MNT	AA	22	1	1	0	2	2	13	4	1	2.8	13.8	20	45%	.158
2017	DUR	AAA	22	12	8	0	24	24	123^2	130	11	2.3	11.1	152	42%	.366
2019	TBA	MLB	24	3	2	0	8	8	40	38	5	2.9	9.1	40	36%	.297

Breakout: 12%   Improve: 27%   Collapse: 13%   Attrition: 26%   MLB: 46%
Comparables: Adam Morgan, Kyle Gibson, Edwar Cabrera

Honeywell underwent Tommy John surgery in February and did not throw a meaningful pitch all year. The early injury, however, means an earlier return for 2019. Prior to going under the knife, Honeywell was a rare five-pitch prospect with excellent control, ranking among the elite pitching prospects in baseball. There's optimism that he'll regain most, if not all, of the effectiveness of his fastball, changeup, slider, curveball and screwball. The biggest challenge will be recapturing that plus control, the piece of the puzzle that typically comes last in recovery. The Rays are hoping he can find it sooner rather than later and join the big-league rotation some time in the middle of the summer.

YEAR	TEAM	LVL	AGE	WHIP	ERA	DRA	WARP	MPH	FB%	WHF	CSP
2016	PCH	A+	21	0.96	2.41	2.35	2.0				
2016	MNT	AA	21	1.10	2.28	4.70	0.3				
2017	MNT	AA	22	0.62	2.08	0.47	0.7				
2017	DUR	AAA	22	1.30	3.64	3.37	3.2				
2019	TBA	MLB	24	1.29	3.84	4.33	0.5				

Matthew Liberatore LHP
Born: 11/06/99   Age: 19   Bats: L   Throws: L
Height: 6'5"   Weight: 200   Origin: Round 1, 2018 Draft (#16 overall)

YEAR	TEAM	LVL	AGE	W	L	SV	G	GS	IP	H	HR	BB/9	K/9	K	GB%	BABIP
2018	RAY	RK	18	1	2	0	8	8	27²	16	0	3.6	10.4	32	45%	.258
2019	TBA	MLB	19	1	3	0	8	8	31¹	31	4	6.8	8.0	28	43%	.296

Comparables: Jaime Barria, Raul Alcantara, Jason Garcia

The Rays were ecstatic to see Liberatore slide to them at pick 16 last June. At one point in consideration for the no. 1 overall pick, signability was a concern for some teams. Tampa Bay not only selected him, but was able to sign him, too. He's long and left-handed with the potential for three plus pitches and some room to grow physically. Typically the Rays like to slow roast their prospects, but Liberatore has an advanced feel for his craft and could head straight to a full-season affiliate if the organization wants to show a little aggression.

YEAR	TEAM	LVL	AGE	WHIP	ERA	DRA	WARP	MPH	FB%	WHF	CSP
2018	RAY	RK	18	0.98	0.98	3.07	0.9				
2019	TBA	MLB	19	1.76	5.93	6.44	-0.3				

Shane McClanahan   LHP

Born: 04/28/97   Age: 22   Bats: L   Throws: L
Height: 6'1"   Weight: 188   Origin: Round 1C, 2018 Draft (#31 overall)

YEAR	TEAM	LVL	AGE	W	L	SV	G	GS	IP	H	HR	BB/9	K/9	K	GB%	BABIP
2019	TBA	MLB	22	2	3	0	8	8	33^1	29	3	5.1	8.1	30	45%	.271

Breakout: 4%   Improve: 4%   Collapse: 0%   Attrition: 2%   MLB: 4%
Comparables: Clay Holmes, Edward Paredes, Elvin Ramirez

Despite picking 16th and 31st, the Rays landed two of the top left-handed pitchers in the 2018 draft class. After nabbing prep arm Matthew Liberatore earlier in the round, Tampa Bay stayed close to home by drafting McClanahan out of nearby University of South Florida. He tossed just seven innings after signing, but the extremely early returns were impressive. The southpaw has an upper-90s fastball with a changeup and curveball that should be above-average as well. He's a bit undersized, so workload will be something to watch as he develops.

YEAR	TEAM	LVL	AGE	WHIP	ERA	DRA	WARP	MPH	FB%	WHF	CSP
2019	TBA	MLB	22	1.45	4.55	4.93	0.2				

Brendan McKay   LHP

Born: 12/18/95   Age: 23   Bats: L   Throws: L
Height: 6'2"   Weight: 212   Origin: Round 1, 2017 Draft (#4 overall)

YEAR	TEAM	LVL	AGE	W	L	SV	G	GS	IP	H	HR	BB/9	K/9	K	GB%	BABIP
2017	HUD	A-	21	1	0	0	6	6	20	10	3	2.2	9.4	21	53%	.159
2018	BGR	A	22	2	0	0	6	6	24^2	8	1	0.7	14.6	40	63%	.167
2018	PCH	A+	22	3	2	0	11	9	47^2	45	2	2.1	10.2	54	39%	.350
2019	TBA	MLB	23	3	4	0	17	12	52^2	47	8	3.4	9.5	56	42%	.288

Breakout: 8%   Improve: 11%   Collapse: 3%   Attrition: 9%   MLB: 17%
Comparables: Matt Bowman, Jake McGee, Eric Surkamp

The first legitimate two-way player drafted in decades, McKay watched Shohei Otani put the blueprint together for a player to hit and pitch for a major-league team. McKay was a top-five pick and played at a major university, but the Rays have brought him along relatively slowly considering his age and experience. A few non-threatening injuries have also slowed the process. As it stands, the former Louisville Cardinal is much farther down the line as a pitcher than he is as a hitter, where he's yet to display that 20-homer potential he was projected to have. On the other hand, McKay the pitcher has been dominant. The organization was already cautious in his usage, but that was not enough to prevent multiple oblique injuries that cost him development. Although his pitching is way ahead of his hitting, the Rays will let him play both ways until it looks like he cannot.

YEAR	TEAM	LVL	AGE	WHIP	ERA	DRA	WARP	MPH	FB%	WHF	CSP
2017	HUD	A-	21	0.75	1.80	3.10	0.5				
2018	BGR	A	22	0.41	1.09	2.63	0.8				
2018	PCH	A+	22	1.17	3.21	3.05	1.2				
2019	TBA	MLB	23	1.28	4.26	4.62	0.5				

Colin Poche LHP

Born: 01/17/94 Age: 25 Bats: L Throws: L
Height: 6'3" Weight: 185 Origin: Round 14, 2016 Draft (#419 overall)

YEAR	TEAM	LVL	AGE	W	L	SV	G	GS	IP	H	HR	BB/9	K/9	K	GB%	BABIP
2016	YAK	A-	22	1	2	0	21	4	31	20	2	4.9	10.5	36	41%	.265
2017	KNC	A	23	2	0	1	13	0	24^2	16	0	2.2	16.1	44	40%	.372
2017	VIS	A+	23	1	1	2	18	0	25^2	14	0	4.6	13.0	37	43%	.275
2018	WTN	AA	24	0	0	1	9	0	11	3	0	1.6	18.8	23	8%	.250
2018	DUR	AAA	24	5	0	1	28	2	50	29	2	3.1	14.0	78	28%	.297
2019	TBA	MLB	25	1	1	0	26	0	27	22	4	4.9	11.7	35	34%	.294

Breakout: 15% Improve: 25% Collapse: 11% Attrition: 31% MLB: 46%
Comparables: Anthony Slama, Donnie Joseph, Michael Schwimer

Pet cat alert. Poche will be a statistical darling in 2019, when he's expected to make his MLB debut. Acquired from the Diamondbacks as a player to be named later in the Steven Souza trade, the lefty has an absurd 1.47 ERA and 227 strikeouts in 147 pro innings while moving quickly through the ranks. Poche does all this without much explanation. He's not an oddity in terms of delivery and he does not throw much harder than the average pitcher. The fastball is low-to-mid 90s, nothing special, but Poche hides the ball well before getting excellent extension. Hitters lose sight of it and then they see it coming much closer than anticipated, which plays up the modest velocity. Poche paired that with a slider in the past, but added a curveball last season to give himself more of an up-and-down game as he likes the fastball elevated. A starter in college, 24 of his 40 appearances last season generated four or more outs, including two test runs as an opener in Durham.

YEAR	TEAM	LVL	AGE	WHIP	ERA	DRA	WARP	MPH	FB%	WHF	CSP
2016	YAK	A-	22	1.19	3.19	2.96	0.8				
2017	KNC	A	23	0.89	1.09	1.84	0.9				
2017	VIS	A+	23	1.05	1.40	2.51	0.7				
2018	WTN	AA	24	0.45	0.00	0.52	0.6				
2018	DUR	AAA	24	0.92	1.08	2.72	1.4				
2019	TBA	MLB	25	1.36	3.99	4.43	0.2				

Tampa Bay Rays 2019

LINEOUTS

Hitters

HITTER	POS	TEAM	LVL	AGE	PA	R	2B	3B	HR	RBI	BB	K	SB	CS	AVG/OBP/SLG	DRC+	WARP
Ryan Boldt	OF	MNT	AA	23	273	40	12	6	7	34	24	58	12	2	.274/.348/.461	131	1.1
Tanner Dodson	OF	HUD	A-	21	224	30	7	3	2	19	20	34	8	3	.273/.344/.369	117	0.4
Lucius Fox	SS	PCH	A+	20	404	54	17	1	2	30	42	79	23	7	.282/.371/.353	124	1.8
	SS	MNT	AA	20	120	14	3	1	1	9	8	20	6	2	.221/.284/.298	70	-0.1
Tyler Frank	INF	HUD	A-	21	226	37	14	1	2	22	33	28	3	3	.288/.425/.412	170	1.8
Joe McCarthy	1B	DUR	AAA	24	191	31	13	1	8	25	25	43	3	1	.269/.377/.513	132	0.6
David Rodriguez	C	PCH	A+	22	117	18	8	1	2	20	8	23	1	0	.317/.385/.471	145	0.7
	C	MNT	AA	22	276	23	13	1	4	44	21	59	2	1	.230/.286/.337	75	-0.8
Nick Schnell	OF	RAY	Rk	18	82	8	4	1	1	4	14	23	2	6	.239/.378/.373	115	-0.4
Jake Smolinski	CF	OAK	MLB	29	41	2	1	1	0	2	1	10	1	0	.128/.171/.205	66	0.0
	CF	NAS	AAA	29	145	25	4	0	10	19	18	42	1	0	.278/.372/.548	139	0.7
Kean Wong	2B	DUR	AAA	23	502	65	23	3	9	50	40	112	7	3	.282/.345/.406	114	1.8

Ryan Boldt, a 2016 second-round pick, upped his power at Double-A and was named to the Southern League All-Star team before a season-ending injury in June. ⚾ His upside is likely higher as a pitcher, but 2018 second-round pick **Tanner Dodson** also fared well as a center fielder in his dual-role pro debut after hitting .310 in two seasons playing both ways at Cal. He lacks power, but Dodson is a switch-hitter with good plate discipline and enough speed to be an asset defensively. ⚾ **Lucius Fox** hasn't hit for any power yet, but he draws walks, steals bases and is the best defensive shortstop in the Rays' system. ⚾ Overshadowed in high school by no. 5 overall pick Jonathan India, **Tyler Frank** went off the board 51 spots later after starring at Florida Atlantic. Primarily a shortstop, he also caught some in college and could wind up in a do-everything role. ⚾ **Joe McCarthy** was limited to 47 games due to a back injury and then suffered a broken hand in the Arizona Fall League. He gets a mulligan in 2019. ⚾ Once an offensive prospect, **David Rodriguez** is still around because of his defense behind the plate. ⚾ Drafted 32nd overall and signed away from Louisville for $2.3 million, **Nick Schnell** has a chance to develop into a middle-of-the-order bat in an outfield corner. ⚾ **Jake Smolinski** is an adequate fifth outfielder who hasn't stayed healthy and should not be allowed to bat against righties. He's also the player who looks most like Taylor Lautner, which should count for more than it does. ⚾ The 13th overall pick in the 2015 draft, **Garrett Whitley** missed the entire 2018 season with a torn labrum. ⚾ Brother Kolton was big mad when **Keon Wong** did not get a September call-up. No word on how he felt about him not being added to the 40-man roster this winter.

Pitchers

PITCHER	TEAM	LVL	AGE	W	L	SV	G	GS	IP	H	HR	BB/9	K/9	K	GB%	WHIP	ERA	DRA	WARP
Anthony Banda	TBA	MLB	24	1	0	0	3	1	14^2	12	1	1.8	6.1	10	49%	1.02	3.68	4.75	0.1
	DUR	AAA	24	4	3	0	8	8	42	43	3	3.9	10.5	49	40%	1.45	3.64	3.83	0.8
Tyler Cloyd	MIA	MLB	31	0	0	0	7	0	17^2	25	3	5.1	6.6	13	32%	1.98	8.66	7.32	-0.5
	NWO	AAA	31	6	5	0	17	15	85^1	96	14	1.9	7.2	68	40%	1.34	5.17	4.11	1.4
Tanner Dodson	HUD	A-	21	1	0	1	9	0	25	12	0	1.8	9.0	25	57%	0.68	1.44	2.62	0.7
Wilmer Font	LAN	MLB	28	0	2	0	6	0	10^1	18	5	0.9	6.1	7	42%	1.84	11.32	7.05	-0.2
	OAK	MLB	28	0	0	0	4	0	6^2	13	5	5.4	12.1	9	33%	2.55	14.85	3.80	0.1
	TBA	MLB	28	2	1	0	9	5	27	15	2	3.7	6.7	20	45%	0.96	1.67	6.46	-0.4
Andrew Kittredge	DUR	AAA	28	6	0	2	21	1	46	41	3	2.3	11.3	58	39%	1.15	2.74	1.94	1.7
	TBA	MLB	28	3	2	0	33	3	38^1	54	7	4.0	7.0	30	51%	1.85	7.75	6.06	-0.5
Adam Kolarek	DUR	AAA	29	5	1	4	31	1	44^2	35	1	2.4	10.5	52	64%	1.05	1.61	3.25	1.0
	TBA	MLB	29	1	0	2	31	0	34^1	38	0	1.3	5.0	19	59%	1.25	3.93	4.25	0.3
Rollie Lacy	SBN	A	22	4	1	0	16	10	71^1	54	3	2.5	10.6	84	64%	1.04	2.02	3.19	1.6
	MYR	A+	22	1	1	0	2	2	9^1	11	2	3.9	9.6	10	59%	1.61	5.79	3.86	0.2
	DEB	A+	22	1	2	0	6	6	28^1	26	1	4.1	8.6	27	56%	1.38	4.45	4.37	0.3
Resly Linares	BGR	A	20	7	3	0	17	17	84^1	69	6	2.7	10.4	97	43%	1.11	3.20	3.56	1.6
Michael Mercado	HUD	A-	19	1	2	0	11	11	50	55	6	2.9	6.8	38	52%	1.42	5.22	3.68	0.9
Ryan Merritt	COH	AAA	26	3	3	0	15	13	71^1	82	10	0.3	6.6	52	46%	1.18	3.79	4.12	1.1
Hoby Milner	PHI	MLB	27	0	0	0	10	0	4^2	6	1	5.8	7.7	4	41%	1.93	7.71	8.40	-0.2
	LEH	AAA	27	0	0	0	25	0	26^1	21	2	4.8	9.6	28	46%	1.33	2.39	3.86	0.4
	DUR	AAA	27	1	0	2	15	1	14^1	14	1	1.9	13.2	21	43%	1.19	3.77	3.40	0.3
	TBA	MLB	27	0	0	0	4	0	2^2	3	2	6.8	13.5	4	14%	1.88	6.75	9.61	-0.1
Andrew Moore	ARK	AA	24	3	1	0	9	9	50^1	38	6	2.5	8.4	47	35%	1.03	3.04	4.96	0.2
	DUR	AAA	24	6	7	0	17	15	83	90	15	3.1	5.7	53	33%	1.43	4.34	6.95	-1.3
Tobias Myers	BGR	A	19	10	6	0	23	21	119	127	11	3.1	7.6	101	36%	1.41	3.71	5.14	0.0
Austin Pruitt	DUR	AAA	28	3	0	1	14	4	39^2	26	2	1.6	11.1	49	49%	0.83	2.95	2.06	1.5
	TBA	MLB	28	2	3	4	23	0	69^2	72	7	2.1	5.4	42	50%	1.26	4.65	3.66	1.0
Chaz Roe	TBA	MLB	31	1	3	1	61	0	50^1	35	6	2.9	9.5	53	48%	1.01	3.58	3.71	0.7
Casey Sadler	PIT	MLB	27	0	0	0	2	0	4^1	9	0	6.2	6.2	3	58%	2.77	8.31	5.04	0.0
	IND	AAA	27	6	5	1	27	8	77	79	7	3.0	7.1	61	46%	1.36	3.39	4.16	1.1
Luis Santos	TOR	MLB	27	1	1	0	15	1	20	26	4	4.5	10.8	24	30%	1.80	7.20	4.00	0.2
	BUF	AAA	27	2	3	0	20	2	42^2	41	2	2.7	8.4	40	33%	1.27	2.74	3.74	0.7

Acquired from Arizona in the Steven Souza swap, **Anthony Banda** had Tommy John surgery in the middle of last season and may miss 2019 as well. ⓧ In the 2014 version of this tome, **Tyler Cloyd**'s usefulness was positioned as "a warm-blooded mammal capable of hurling a small sphere in the vicinity of a pentagon placed on the surface of the Earth, with little value beyond that." Not much has changed. ⓧ Acquired from the Dodgers for Logan Forsythe after the Twins turned them down for Brian Dozier, **Jose De Leon** had his Tommy John surgery early enough to potentially make it back to the majors in 2019. ⚾ Drafted out of Cal as a legitimate two-way player, 2018 second-round pick **Tanner Dodson** is considered a better prospect on the mound and showed why as he dominated the New York-Penn League. He closed in college and worked as a multi-inning reliever in his pro debut, but Dodson has the secondary offerings to potentially start. ⚾ Traded on April 25 and then again on May 25, **Wilmer Font** showed some promise with the Rays before getting hurt in June and missing the rest of the season. ⚾ Cuban signee **Sandy Gaston** received a $2.6 million bonus for throwing the ball insanely hard for a 16-year-old. ⚾ **Andrew Kittredge** struggled in every role for the Rays in 2018 and also looks like he needs sleep in every photo. ⚾ **Adam Kolarek** is a viable second lefty in the pen with good control, but seems destined to be an up-and-down arm. ⚾ With Eddie Butler's poor performance, the onus falls on **Rollie Lacy** to be the return for the Cole Hamels trade. Ooh, *ouch*, it looks like that onus hit him pretty squarely. Rollie? Buddy? Are you oka— ahh, okay, yeah. He says he's fine. ⚾ A finesse lefty with a chance to grow into more, **Resly Linares** signed with the Rays for $275,000 in the same international class as Jesus Sanchez and Diego Castillo. ⚾ The Rays' second-round pick in 2017, right-hander **Michael Mercado**, struggled in his short-season assignment. ⚾ **Ryan Merritt** is a nice emergency starter, but there's a reason the left-hander and his high-80s fastball haven't had a chance to do more than that so far. ⚾ If you're going to play baseball and be named **Hoby Milner**, you pretty much have to be one of a) a glove-first middle infielder, b) a journeyman LOOGY, c) a bullpen catcher. Our protagonist chose door no. 2. ⚾ **Andrew Moore** may or may not be allowed in Canada. He will definitely need to pitch better to justify continuing to hold a 40-man roster spot. ⚾ **Tobias Myers**, acquired from the Orioles for Tim Beckham in mid-2017, has the potential to be a quality starter with three above-average pitches. ⚾ Now entering the game, **Austin Pruitt**. If you hear this in the ballpark, you can leave. If you hear this on the television at home, go spend time with your family. ⚾ **Chaz Roe** threw his slider 53 percent of the time last season, topping 50 innings in the majors for the first time at age 31. The slider is good, and he leans on the side of ground balls, but without much else he's limited to the platoon advantage. ⚾ **Casey Sadler** missed all of 2016 after Tommy John surgery and spent almost two full seasons working his way back to form in the minors. He could still be a useful major-league piece but, at 28, time is running out. ⚾ Giving up homers is a thing that happens when you don't have elite stuff or strong command. Giving up homers with two strikes, like **Luis Santos** did 75 percent of the time last season, is a thing that gets you sent back to Triple-A.

Rays Prospects

The State of the System:
The Rays have built a deep, balanced organization. This is one of the best farm systems in baseball.

The Top Ten:

1. Wander Franco   SS   OFP: 70   Likely: 60
ETA: Late 2020 or after Super 2 in 2021
Born: 03/01/01   Age: 18   Bats: B   Throws: R   Height: 5'10"   Weight: 189
Origin: International Free Agent, 2017

The Report: I told the staff at the beginning of this year's list process that I wanted to keep these reports to 150-200 words, so "please try to keep them under 400." But to paraphrase Blaise Pascal, I have only made this report longer because I have not the time to make it shorter. Franco is a potential 6/6 offensive shortstop; those hit and power grades might be light. He has a bit of a dip/hitch to his load, but the bat speed is so good it doesn't matter. It's plus-plus, and he can let pitches really eat before he triggers. He knows the zone well already, recognizes spin, doesn't sell out for power. The raw power is plus. The game power will be plus. The ball makes *that* sound off the bat.

Despite a frame that elicited a scout quote of "he's kind of a block," Franco has enough present athletic tools to project as a shortstop in the majors. He likely won't be a regular at 7:55 PM on ESPN for Web Gems (man, is Baseball Tonight even still on?), but he's a rangy up-the-middle type with good hands and above-average arm strength. The arm grade can play down as he can get a bit scattershot on the move. He struggles with game speed at times, but I expect the defensive issues to get ironed out with further reps. He'd be a plus defender at second base if he does have to move. He's an above-average runner at present although I'd expect him to slow down to average in his 20s. Okay, the second half of this blurb isn't as exciting, so let's circle back to the bat. It makes Franco one of the elite prospects in the game, and as I said in his eyewitness from last summer, stuff him to all your friends.

The Risks: High. There was an argument to go 80/60 extreme on Franco. It's not a grade I really like to use, but we've had internal discussions about using it before; it's on the table. There were two issues with this. (1) I didn't quite see enough from him to go the full OFP 80… yet. (2) I don't see him as an extreme risk. The bat is that good and even a "generous" physical projection coupled with his defensive tools would make him an above-average second base glove. So 70/60 high it is. This may end up looking needlessly conservative too. No question about it, this is a fun gig.

Ben Carsley's Fantasy Take: Seems… pretty good! Given the premium hit tool, the chance for plus power and the fact that Franco will also run a little bit to start his career, it seems the only real flaw in his profile is that he'll grow up to be a Ray (that is one of only three digs I'm allowing myself this article, I promise). It'd be nice if Franco was a year-or-so closer, but he's a no-doubt top-25 dynasty prospect at this point, and he's on the short list of guys who could rank 1-1 a year from now. If visions of a Xander Bogaerts-like outcome are spinning in your head, well, it's tough to blame you.

2. Brent Honeywell   RHP
OFP: 70   Likely: 55   ETA: 2019
Born: 03/31/95   Age: 24   Bats: R   Throws: R   Height: 6'2"   Weight: 180
Origin: Round 2, 2014 Draft (#72 overall)

The Report: Honeywell was one of several high-end pitching prospects to come down with a torn UCL shortly after arriving at camp last February. He was set to compete for a major-league rotation spot (lol j/k he wasn't coming up until the end of April… maybe), coming off a dominant 2017 in the upper minors. He missed all of 2018, but is throwing off a mound again, and should be ready around Memorial Day, depending on how his rehab goes. So there isn't much to change in the report this year. Well, at least we don't have any new info one way or the other. Surgery can change things. But assuming Honeywell's stuff comes back, he will quickly be one of the best pitching prospects in baseball again, and quickly after that, a major-league starter. He's shown plus velocity and five pitches in total that project as average or better, so it doesn't even have to come all the way back for him to be an effective pitcher.

The Risks: High. This is the default "dude hasn't thrown a pro pitch since Tommy John" risk.

Ben Carsley's Fantasy Take: This tends to happen to a few pitchers we rank every year—last year it was Honeywell and A.J. Puk, this year it will be Michael Kopech—but when a great arm like this gets TJ, we basically just lock their value in as-is and add in a half-tick of risk. That means Honeywell should be in the conversation once more for a top-25 spot on our dynasty top-101, although his lack of truly elite fantasy upside may push him a little lower. That being said, assuming he's healthy, he's among the best bets in the minors to at least surface as a reliable fantasy SP3/4, and there's always the chance for a little more.

3. Jesus Sanchez   OF
OFP: 60   Likely: 50   ETA: Early 2020
Born: 10/07/97   Age: 21   Bats: L   Throws: R   Height: 6'3"   Weight: 210
Origin: International Free Agent, 2014

The Report: Sanchez has one of the most projectable frames in baseball and a potential plus hit/power combo, but the on-field performance didn't quite match the tools in 2018. You'd be forgiven for wanting to continue betting on that sweet lefty swing though, or that a dozen or so of his 30+ doubles will turn into home runs as he fills out. Sanchez's swing has plenty of lift, and there's enough present bat control to project him getting most of that plus raw power into games. He tends to have an overly expansive view of what he actually can hit though, and his aggressive approach got undone in a brief AA cameo. He's also already primarily a right fielder, and while—in 2018 at least—that might have partially been due to wanting to get Joshua Lowe as many of the center field reps as possible, Sanchez is ticketed for a corner regardless. That puts pressure on the bat to play to projection, but it's a bet we're willing to make.

The Risks: Medium. It's a corner outfield profile with a power projection bet and some brief Double-A struggles in 2018. So it's not exactly "safe," as much as we like the bat.

Ben Carsley's Fantasy Take: Sanchez's upside may be a bit oversold in some dynasty circles—he's not the next great outfield prospect—but he's a reasonably safe bet to at least become a fantasy OF4/5, and there's a definite OF3 ceiling to boot. In his early days or off years, Sanchez could hit .270 or so with 15-20 homers and solid but unremarkable RBI/run totals. In his best years, look for 2018 Eddie Rosario (.288/323/.479 with 24 homers) as a solid statistical comp. Add in a reasonable timetable (even factoring in the Rays' conservative approach) and you get a top-50 dynasty prospect.

Brendan McKay   1B   OFP: 60   Likely: 50
ETA: 2020; the pitching prospect here will be ready in 2019.
Born: 12/18/95   Age: 23   Bats: L   Throws: L   Height: 6'2"   Weight: 212
Origin: Round 1, 2017 Draft (#4 overall)

The Report: Shohei Ohtani came to the majors as a fully-formed two-way threat. With Brendan McKay, we get to watch the actual developmental process on both sides. It's made him, uh, a difficult prospect to grade and rank through our normal channels. The pitching side is fairly easy to deal with. McKay flashed a little more velocity in 2018, making the fastball comfortably plus. He has a major-league ready above-average slider, a potentially average curve and change, and feel and command for everything. While he doesn't have huge upside as a starter, he might be in the majors already if he was solely a pitcher.

As a hitter, it's tough to discern much from a major college bat playing three days a week in A-ball as a 22-year-old. He has the raw power and approach to be a viable 1B/DH option on his off days, but he's unlikely to be an Ohtani-level force at the plate. There's ways to leverage that of course, but he wouldn't be a 101 guy as a hitter. It does save a roster spot, and it's really neat. You can make an argument McKay is one of the most talented baseball prospects in the minors, but we have to project "actual major-league role outside of the talent vacuum" more here than usual.

There's also added development risk and lead time. The oblique injury that sidelined him for six weeks in 2018 is an example. Things you could maybe play through, you can't pitch through. McKay is already 23 and didn't hit so well in Charlotte that you'd move him to Double-A on his performance there alone, even if the arm almost demands it. Perhaps 2019 and the upper minors will clarify things. Perhaps not.

The Risks: Low and High, sort of. He's a very polished pitcher and would be a Top 101 prospect just on the arm, but the dual development path makes things slower and riskier.

Ben Carsley's Fantasy Take: McKay might be a fine MLB prospect, but for my money he's among the more overrated plays in dynasty. Now that we project the bat to be more "nice for a team to have" than "everyday first baseman" quality, we're looking at a fantasy SP4/5 who may be able to occasionally add a little bit of offensive value depending on your league format. Given his proximity to the majors and his floor, that might be enough to get McKay on the 101, but he won't sniff the top-50. If someone still wants to treat him as one of the game's elite prospects thanks to his name value and draft slot, you should be willing to move him.

5 Lucius Fox SS

OFP: 60   Likely: 50   ETA: Early 2020
Born: 07/02/97   Age: 21   Bats: B   Throws: R   Height: 6'1"   Weight: 180
Origin: International Free Agent, 2015

The Report: I couldn't stop Jarrett from putting a Batman reference in the Annual w/r/t Fox, but we will play it straight here. Fox is a speedy, slick-fielding shortstop, a lock to stick at the 6 and a potential plus glove there. He's a 70 runner who was marginally more efficient on the bases in 2018, even if he's still a bit raw there. He should continue to get opportunities to steal though due to a potential plus hit tool and a good approach at the plate.

The obvious flaw here is—Bahamian Home Run Derby captainship aside—a distinct lack of power. A wide base and simple weight transfer, coupled with a slight, but athletic frame, doesn't bode much for additional power projection either. Upper minors pitching may challenge him more and cut into that walk rate as well. As long as Fox can line enough balls over the infielders' heads, the glove and speed will carry the rest of the profile. If not, he will end up as more of a utility infielder.

The Risks: Medium. As good as that glove is, Fox has to show enough with the stick in the upper minors before we fully buy into a plus everyday profile.

Ben Carsley's Fantasy Take: Fox may not have a very exciting fantasy profile, but he's got a useful one. Even if Fox never truly clicks offensively and becomes a down-the-order slap hitter, his glove and speed should keep him in the lineup often enough to threaten for around 30 steals a year. That'd make him worthy of a bench spot in just about any league, and it makes him a starter in deeper formats. Add in the upside—that Fox may grow into solid averages and play every day—and he's probably a top-101 prospect, albeit more because of the scarcity of stolen bases than anything else. Also, spying on 30 million people isn't part of his job description.

6 Shane Baz   RHP   OFP: 60   Likely: 50   ETA: 2023
Born: 06/17/99   Age: 20   Bats: R   Throws: R   Height: 6'3"   Weight: 190
Origin: Round 1, 2017 Draft (#12 overall)

The Report: Although he has mostly just held serve from his status/report last year as the 12th overall pick and a back end 101 prospect, Baz was a heckuva player to be named later in the Archer deal. He still offers mid-90s heat and a potential plus slider, albeit amidst outstanding questions about his delivery and third pitch. Baz has a full four-pitch mix with both the change and curve having a chance to get to average. The arm action is compact, but high effort, and the delivery has the kind of late torque you associate with fringy command projection, or perhaps a move to the pen. Baz has an electric arm though, and the upside in the profile makes him one of the most intriguing teenage arms in baseball.

The Risks: High. Third pitch and command questions, only a short-season track record.

Ben Carsley's Fantasy Take: We may have been a bit too aggressive on Baz when we ranked him 57th overall in last season's top-101, but Baz still has Great Stuff™ and a promising ceiling as a fantasy SP3/4. The lead time and solid-but-not great ceiling should conspire to lower him in the rankings this time around, but he's still got an outside shot at making our newest iteration of the top-101.

7 Vidal Brujan   2B   OFP: 60   Likely: 50   ETA: 2021
Born: 02/09/98   Age: 21   Bats: B   Throws: R   Height: 5'9"   Weight: 155
Origin: International Free Agent, 2014

The Report: Brujan's elite speed has been his calling card since signing out of the Dominican Republic in 2015. As a second baseman with no other standout tool, however, he was often overlooked in our world. That changed last season, as the bat took a major step forward and he slashed .320/.403/.459 across two levels.

Brujan is aggressive at the plate but has above-average contact ability and a solid understanding of the strike zone. His swing stays in the zone for a long time and he adjusts well to secondaries. While not a huge part of his game, there is some sneaky power generated by above-average bat speed. He's aggressive on the bases and has double-plus raw speed. Defensively, Brujan is limited to second base. He's raw there but his natural athleticism suggests he'll eventually become adequate. The bat and speed portend a future everyday major-leaguer at the keystone.

The Risks: High. His defensive limitations put pressure on the bat to excel. He made the Midwest League look easy but will have to prove it at every level.

Ben Carsley's Fantasy Take: Wow, my love of speedy middle infielders matches up against my hatred of the Rays. A true unstoppable force vs. immovable object scenario for ya boy here. Honestly, Brujan's profile isn't widely dissimilar to what Jose Peraza's was as a prospect (except Brujan is even more limited defensively), and we all know what I thought of the Brave-turned-Dodger-turned-Red. Peraza may not be lighting the world on fire, but he's actually been a pretty useful fantasy piece thanks to his speed. Brujan could profile similarly, though there's always the risk that his limitations will conspire to push him to a bench role. Overall the profile is limited enough that it may keep him off the top-101, but then again we do love speed…

8. Matthew Liberatore LHP
OFP: 60 Likely: 50 ETA: 2022
Born: 11/06/99 Age: 19 Bats: L Throws: L Height: 6'5" Weight: 200
Origin: Round 1, 2018 Draft (#16 overall)

The Report: Liberatore was one of the top players available in last June's draft. He's a big lefty with three potential plus pitches and smooth, if somewhat inconsistent mechanics. He fell to the 16th pick for reasons we can't entirely explain, where the Rays were quite happy to snap him up. If there was a perceived signability problem, it didn't manifest, because he signed for slightly under the slot value even though he was taken a dozen picks later than expected.

Liberatore was in discussion to make the 101 until the very end of the process. We broadly agree that he was the best prep pitcher out of last year's draft right now. This is probably the deepest system in baseball for this particular grade level. And when in doubt, we're going to give the edge to players with more of a substantive track record than high school showcases, some short stints in the complex, and one game in the Appy. The difference between 3-10 in this system isn't huge on talent.

The Risks: Extreme. He's a prep pitcher. His fastball velocity has never been consistent and dipped after the draft, which is both entirely normal for prep pitchers transitioning to pro ball and a reason everyone in the industry has been talking about the volatility inherent in drafting prep pitchers for the last several decades.

Ben Carsley's Fantasy Take: Liberatore has more name value than actual dynasty value right now thanks to his draft slot. If you want to call him a top-150 guy because he's left-handed with solid-average upside, knock yourself out. But don't kid yourself into thinking he's a top-101 (or better) guy yet.

9 **Brandon Lowe 2B**   OFP: 55   Likely: 50   ETA: Debuted in 2018
Born: 07/06/94   Age: 24   Bats: L   Throws: R   Height: 6'0"   Weight: 185
Origin: Round 3, 2015 Draft (#87 overall)

The Report: Lowe remains eligible for this list by exactly one at-bat after torching the high minors in 2018 and punching his ticket to TPA. The swing changes he made last year continued to pay dividends with added power to his profile in 2018. It's a leg kick and lift swing from a shorter middle infielder with good knowledge of the strike zone. You know how this can sometimes go. Lowe is stocky and strong and the power can play line-to-line despite only average bat speed. The swing can get a bit stiff as well, and he's going to be susceptible to better stuff down. This may mean more strikeouts and worse overall quality of contact against major-league arms, but Lowe shows enough feel for hitting to get most of this newfound power into games.

Everything else in the profile is average. He's limited to second base as any sort of regular, but should be fine there. The hit tool is going to be the ultimate arbiter of how this all plays out, and that kind of profile can be a bit high variance despite the rather stable skill set. Lowe could have some .260, 25 home runs seasons, but they may be mixed in with years where he's more of a platoon bat.

The Risks: Low(e). The Rays have a very crowded infield, but getting Lowe major-league at-bats should be a priority as any more action in Durham is just a waste of time.

Ben Carsley's Fantasy Take: I'll be honest—I suck at evaluating players with this type of profile. Part of me wants to overcompensate and buy in on Lowe since I've missed on similar guys in the past, but at the end of the day his modest upside doesn't justify any sort of heavy encouragement to buy in dynasty leagues. If you already own Lowe, congrats on getting in on the ground floor of a solid asset. If he's already owned, well, I don't think I'd be banging down the door to acquire him. Let's just all hope for a Scooter Gennett sequel while more realistically preparing for something more akin to off-peak Neil Walker.

10 **Ronaldo Hernandez C**   OFP: 55   Likely: 45   ETA: 2021
Born: 11/11/97   Age: 21   Bats: R   Throws: R   Height: 6'1"   Weight: 185
Origin: International Free Agent, 2014

The Report: My first glimpse of Hernandez came this season during the Midwest League All-Star Game home run derby. He went toe to toe with Cleveland's Will Benson, eventually besting the former first-round pick. Hernandez's plus raw power was on display that night, but it was in my later looks where he showed he's more than just a big bat. He has natural bat-to-ball skills and plate discipline that complements his raw strength and plus bat speed. Relatively new to the position, Hernandez has also made great strides defensively. As the year progressed his comfort level as a receiver appeared to increase, and he looked more and more natural behind the dish. He has a strong arm and the physical tools to eventually become a solid major-league backstop.

The Risks: High. He's a young catcher who has yet to face upper level pitching.

Ben Carsley's Fantasy Take: I refuse to let my heart be broken by catching prospects any more, but Hernandez is a good one. With Danny Jansen and Keibert Ruiz both somewhat likely to exhaust their prospect eligibility in the next 18 months, Hernandez is a solid bet for the top dynasty catching prospect thereafter. We're still quite a ways away from that future, however, and Hernandez's lead time and… well… position will likely keep him from top-101 status. He won't miss by much though.

The Next Five:

11
Shane McClanahan   LHP
Born: 04/28/97   Age: 22   Bats: L   Throws: L   Height: 6'1"   Weight: 188
Origin: Round 1C, 2018 Draft (#31 overall)

A lot of what we wrote above with Liberatore applies to McClanahan as well, except the culprit for his draft-day slide is more obvious. He struggled down the stretch of the college season and already has Tommy John on his resume. He's a lefty who throws 100 with two potential above-average secondaries, but there is some violence in his delivery and he has struggled to consistently throw strikes. He fits broadly into the same range as 3-10 as well, albeit with more health and reliever risk. I would expect the Rays to try to keep him in the rotation as long as possible, but he could move very quickly as a reliever if Tampa were so inclined.

12
Nathaniel Lowe   1B
Born: 07/07/95   Age: 23   Bats: L   Throws: R   Height: 6'4"   Weight: 235
Origin: Round 13, 2016 Draft (#390 overall)

Now we shift gears to a more common archetype of our first twenty lists this year—and really, every list, every year—the slugging first base prospect. Lowe #2 had a breakout year in 2018, slugging 27 home runs and posting a better than 10% walk rate across three levels. He is already 23, and was a 13th round draft pick out of Mississippi State, so his age and pedigree aren't going to wow you. But you can't argue with the production.

With these profiles the question is always: "But will he hit enough in the majors?" It's a length and strength swing to get to his borderline plus-plus raw power, and commensurate stiffness as well. But Lowe isn't merely a one-dimensional slugger, even though I expect any major-league success to look Three True Outcome-ish. He has some feel for hitting and can drive the ball throughout the strike zone. I expect better velocity will beat him more often in the majors, and he's not going to be much more than passable in the field, but he should be able to take up the mantle of league-average Rays first baseman. For a time, at least. They go through them about as often as Spinal Tap cycles through drummers. At least a DFA or trade to Seattle is preferable to being felled by a bizarre gardening accident.

13 Ryan Boldt   OF
Born: 11/22/94   Age: 24   Bats: L   Throws: R   Height: 6'2"   Weight: 210
Origin: Round 2, 2016 Draft (#53 overall)

The Rays depth in potential high-end prospect talent is impressive and arguably the envy of the entire league, but we are entering the likely bench outfielder portion of the list—with an interesting exception to come. Boldt is well on his way to fulfilling that destiny. He played all three outfield positions in the Southern League and is average to perhaps a bit above in center field. At the plate, Boldt offers a simple, compact swing that prioritizes contact over power. He has the usual good Rays prospect approach. Neither the bat nor glove alone suggest a slam dunk everyday guy, but the broad base of skills should keep Boldt in the majors well into the 2020s.

14 Carl Chester   OF
Born: 12/12/95   Age: 23   Bats: R   Throws: R   Height: 6'0"   Weight: 200
Origin: Round 12, 2017 Draft (#349 overall)

We often like to say that these evaluations happen in more or less a vacuum. "What can a player do?" over "What might the organization do with a player?" The Rays can confound that. Partially because of their organizational creativity (aggressive platooning, the opener, signing every former Mariners shortstop prospect), but they also tend to be very conservative w/r/t development tracks for their prospects. Chester landed on the "next ten" of the 2018 Rays prospect list. That's aggressive for a 12th round college pick in a very good system, but the Penn League reports support it. His bat needs to keep developing, of course, but what can you actually learn from a full season in the Midwest League for a 22-year-old out of the University of Miami? His 2018 season was almost a dead ringer for his 2017 junior year at Miami that triggered concerns about his stick. Is the competition really that much better than Friday nights in the ACC?

This is all philosophy in the end. What we do know is he's still a potential plus glove in center with a bat that makes you worry he's a fourth outfielder in the end. We won't learn a whole lot more in Port Charlotte next year, but we'll keep him on the Next Ten until the reports change or we mercifully get too old for this gig ourselves. In a race between the Rays developmental track and the Heat Death of the Universe, we're all winners in the end.

15 Tanner Dodson   RHP
Born: 05/09/97   Age: 22   Bats: B   Throws: R   Height: 6'1"   Weight: 160
Origin: Round 2, 2018 Draft (#71 overall)

The other two-way weapon in the Rays system, Dodson isn't quite as good a prospect in either role, but his skill set might actually be easier to leverage full value out of than McKay's. At the plate he's an athletic, switch-hitting, hit over power center fielder. On the mound he can touch the upper-90s and will flash a plus slider.

The swing is a little stiff from the right side, and his bat speed is fringy, but he controls the barrel well. As a hitting prospect, Dodson would be your standard extra outfielder type, and there's a reason he was seen more as a pitcher coming into the draft. But you can Davey Johnson him, sending him to the outfield for your LOOGY. You won't be hiding him there either, so you can get almost all of his fourth outfielder/relief arm value into games using various machinations.

There is more risk here than with McKay that the bat may not get there in a "major-league hitter" sense, leaving him more of your run-of-the-mill 95-and-a-slider guy. Dodson is probably more fun than good, and almost wasted some in the DH league—although the Rays are the right org to get creative here—but it's good to have fun prospects lying around.

Others of note:

Austin Franklin, RHP, Low-A Bowling Green

Franklin was putting together a nice season anchoring the Bowling Green staff until he went down with an elbow injury in July. When healthy, he features a fastball that currently sits 92-94 but could play up a notch with physical maturity. The curve is his best secondary and has the potential to be a plus offering. It features 12-6 movement, has depth, and Franklin will bury it down and away to righties. There are a lot of moving parts to the delivery and it causes the command to waver at times. He's likely to miss most, if not all, of 2019 and if he can return to form it'll most likely be in relief.

Jose Mujica, RHP, Triple-A Durham

Mujica missed some time with a forearm strain in 2018. While there was no structural damage at the time, it's not exactly a surprise that he got Tommy John surgery shortly after the season ended. It's too bad, as Mujica was knocking on the door of the majors on the strength of his mid-90s fastball and potential above-average slider. His delivery has some effort, and his fastball didn't move a ton—although there was good riding life up and occasional run—so he was likely destined for the pen anyway. Now that timetable gets sets back a year or so, and we will have to see what the stuff looks like in 2020.

Resly Linares, LHP, Low-A Bowling Green

Linares did not have Tommy John surgery in 2018, though he did miss about two months with vague shoulder issues. Pitchers, man. Linares came out the other side fine enough, although his slight frame—talk about the uniform *literally* hanging off a player—is going to lead to continued durability concerns until (if?) he fills out some. The fastball runs between the upper-80s and lower-90s but Linares commands it well to all four quadrants and there's a bit of deception as well.

It's a projectable frame with good arm speed so you'd hope he settles more in the average velocity range as he ages. The curve is potentially above-average, a big, low-70s 1-7 breaker with good tilt, although he will snap it off at times when he wants to spot it. He could use a better changeup, and a few more orders of double meat Chipotle burritos on the road, but Linares is still an arm worth keeping an eye on, even if he's been lost in the shuffle a bit in a top-tier system.

Roberto Alvarez, C, rookie-ball Princeton

Getting overly attached to a prep catcher? That's for amateurs. IFA catchers in their second season in rookie-ball? That's the ticket. It was harder to find a low minors sleeper in the Rays system than you'd think despite the overall org depth, but Alvarez caught my eye due to his advanced offensive tools for an 18-year-old.

He's got above-average raw power and can show it off to the oppo gap already. There's loft and above-average bat speed, and although the swing can be a little stiff, he should get to most of his pop. He doesn't sell out for it, and has an idea at the plate. Right-on-right spin is a significant issue at present, but one you can still chalk up to those awkward teenage years for now.

The defense is also a work in progress. Alvarez can get stabby on the backhand and box pitches a bit, but he's a solid athlete for a catcher, blocks balls well, and flashes an average arm. It's gonna be a long while before he's ready, but he's one to watch as a potential role 5 catcher sometime in the 2020s.

Tommy Romero, RHP, Low-A Bowling Green

There was not a lot to choose from in the Mariners farm system when the Rays sent Denard Span and Alex Colome to Seattle in May. While it was not a sexy return, they did net two potential back end rotation types in Andrew Moore and Tommy Romero. Romero, a former 15th-round pick out of Eastern Florida State, has a thick, solid build and is physically mature. The stuff, while not electric, is effective. The fastball sits in the low-90's but is heavy with run and Romero spots it well in the zone. The changeup is his most advanced secondary. Hitters have a hard time with it as Romero replicates his arm action well and it fades away from righties. He doesn't have a high floor, but Romero is a durable, strike-throwing starter who could eventually find his way onto a big-league pitching staff.

Tampa Bay Rays 2019

Top Talents 25 and Under (born 4/1/93 or later):

1. Willy Adames
2. Wander Franco
3. Tyler Glasnow
4. Austin Meadows
5. Brent Honeywell
6. Jesus Sanchez
7. Brendan McKay
8. Lucius Fox
9. Shane Baz
10. Vidal Brujan

In some ways, this was one of the harder 25 and Under lists to do. Not only are there three fairly recently-graduated top global prospects, but there are another half-dozen players to consider here. Thankfully, the system depth prevents us from having to order them immediately.

Willy Adames is, more or less, what we expected Willy Adames to be right now. He spent years edging up our lists, peaking at No. 14 on the 2018 midseason 50. He mostly just kept drilling in on an above-average outcome every year, and his slash lines have stayed bizarrely consistent across levels and environments, even into the second half of 2018 in the majors. That hides real improvements, because every level is tougher and maintaining your production from Low-A to MLB means you're constantly improving. If he keeps improving in the majors, he could outhit those MILB numbers. Adames edges out Wander Franco by the thinnest of margins in what amounts to a slight stylistic preference for the very good guy who has done it in the majors over the potential superstar who has yet to reach full-season ball yet.

Tyler Glasnow spent the first half of the 2018 season walking too many guys in the Pirates bullpen, and the second half of the season pitching well in Tampa's rotation; DRA suggests that he was actually pretty effective in both roles. He still has an incredible fastball/curveball combination, one of the best in baseball in terms of raw stuff, and absolutely good enough that he can excel in a rotation with little more than a show-me change. All that separates him from a top-of-the-rotation outcome is continuing to throw strikes, but his history throwing strikes is sketchy enough that we want to see it for more than eleven starts before crowning him as such. Glasnow alone has the potential to make the Chris Archer trade look terrible for Pittsburgh.

Austin Meadows is still functionally a prospect, but he accrued a bit too much MLB playing time to remain list-eligible. You know the drill here by now: immense talent, inconsistent results, way too many injuries. Meadows was up-and-down for the Pirates, playing well in MLB stints but struggling in Triple-A, before the Rays picked him up in said Archer trade. He proceeded to torch the International League for the rest of the season and earned his way to St. Pete in September. Meadows is only 23 and he'll probably open the season in the Rays outfield. Like Glasnow, the sky is the limit here.

There are a *lot* of guys who deserve a brief mention here. Former A's first-rounder Daniel Robertson has turned into a really nifty super-utility type, and added a bit of outfield work to his full accoutrement in the infield in 2018. Former Giants first-rounder Christian Arroyo looks like he's headed down the same path, but hasn't quite gotten there yet. Diego Castillo gets it up to 102 MPH and has way more role versatility than we expected he would, everywhere from the first to the ninth. Jose Alvarado touches 101 MPH from the left side and leans on a great slider. Hunter Wood emerged out of obscurity to become a strong bullpen piece who also did some work as The Opener. Jake Faria is a nice back-of-the-rotation type who could be used in a bunch of different roles moving forward. Jalen Beeks came over in the Nathan Eovaldi trade and immediately filled the long relief role that is so crucial for the success of that Opener strategy. Andrew Moore might fill a similar role next year. We haven't even mentioned Anthony Banda yet.

Oh yeah, and AL Cy Young winner Blake Snell only missed this list by four months. The Rays certainly don't lack for young talent.

Part 3: Featured Articles

The Hole in The Shift is Fixing Itself

Russell Carleton

I've been on a bit of a mission against The Shift of late. I'm not out to get The Shift for the usual reasons that people oppose it. The words "the right way to play the game" won't be found on my lips. If a team wants to pursue a strategy that is within the rules and it works, then by all means, they have my blessing (not that they need it). Instead, my concern with The Shift is a worry that it doesn't work, or at least that it has a flaw that needs fixing.

The data show that while The Shift does a decent job of preventing singles on balls in play (what it's supposed to do), it also increases the number of walks that happen in front of it, and the number of additional walks outweighs the number of singles saved. It's a problem because you can't throw a guy out if he gets to walk to first base.

But the "why" was important. It seemed that The Shift was changing the way in which pitchers pitched. We saw that there were fewer fastballs thrown in front of The Shift than we might otherwise expect, and that pitchers tended to stay out of the strike zone a little more. Not by a lot. In fact, it might not even be visible to the naked eye. The percentage of pitches that are out of the zone goes from 51.0 to 53.3 from a standard defense (two right/two left) to a full shift (three on one side). That difference stands up even after we control for the types of hitters that get shifted against. And it's enough to drive up the walk rate to where it cancels out the benefits that teams thought they were getting with The Shift... and then some.

But there was some hope. I found that when individual pitchers stayed closer to the in-zone/out-of-zone mix that they used without The Shift on, they could still get the benefits of The Shift without the walk problems. So, in theory, a team could simply figure out a way to convince its pitchers to not fall prey to the walk trap and The Shift would once again be their friend.

It's reasonable to think that some teams might be more hip to this idea than others. Maybe some figured it out a year before the others. Maybe they were better at getting the message across to their pitchers. Or, maybe no one has figured it out yet.

Warning! Gory Mathematical Details Ahead!

I used data from 2015-2017, made available through MLB's data portal, Baseball Savant. They are kind enough to note when teams are using an infield shift (three fielders on one side of second base), as opposed to a "strategic shift" (someone's playing a bit out of position, but it's not quite that drastic) or a "standard" alignment.

Since we're doing this by team, I can't just look at raw walk rates, because we know that some teams have good pitchers and others have not-so-good pitchers. Some have a mix of both. I used the log-odds ratio method to take into account a batter's general walking proclivities, and a pitcher's as well, and then shoving them into a binary logistic regression. Then, I asked the computer to generate a specific coefficient for each team's pitchers, for when they went into The Shift and how that affected their walk rate.

Using those coefficients, I was able to project what would happen if a league-average pitcher faced a league-average hitter (which we expect would produce a league-average walk rate; from 2015-2017, 7.7 percent of plate appearances ended in a walk) and then just switched his hat. Here's the top five and the bottom five:

Top 5 Teams	Projected Shift Walk Rate	Bottom 5 Teams	Projected Shift Walk Rate
Rockies	6.2%	Rangers	11.2%
Pirates	6.7%	Mets	10.4%
Indians	7.2%	Dodgers	10.2%
Astros	7.3%	Cardinals	9.9%
Braves	7.7%	Tigers	9.7%

There are probably people out there right now trying to figure out what the common thread is among the top and bottom teams. I'm sure, because this is Baseball Prospectus, people are already trying to make the case that sabermetric "early adopters" have some sort of edge here. I think that the more interesting piece is that by the time you get to fifth place in The Shift, we're at league average.

As a sanity check, I examined the issue on a pitch-by-pitch level, looking at how often pitchers threw their pitches in the GameDay strike zone, and again using the same basic methodology and getting team-specific coefficients. The names on the list re-arranged themselves, but the idea was the same, and the two lists correlated with an R of .593.

There's a reason that I don't usually do this type of leaderboard post. I don't really know what the Rockies, Pirates, Indians, Astros, and Braves have in common, or what they have that the bottom five don't. I can put a shrug emoji here and say, "Well, it must be something!" but that seems like a cop-out. Instead, I'd like to present another table and suggest that the table above doesn't even really matter anymore.

Year	League Percent Outside K Zone (Full Shift)	League Percent in K Zone (No Shift)	Difference
2015	54.1%	51.1%	3.0%
2016	53.3%	50.9%	2.4%
2017	52.6%	50.9%	1.7%
2018	52.0%	50.7%	1.3%

The hole in The Shift is fixing itself, and it's coming down really fast league wide. In my earlier work on The Shift, I suggested that until teams stopped having such a huge difference between their out-of-zone rate with and without The Shift on, there would just be too many walks for The Shift to make sense. It seems that all 30 of them have been working toward just that. I once estimated that it takes about 10 years for an idea to filter its way through baseball. At this rate, it looks like teams are going to catch up a lot faster than that. And yeah, they're all saber-smart now.

It's likely that whatever magic it was that the Rockies and Pirates had has made its way to Texas and Queens. Or is at least on its way. And if teams are committing to fixing the walk problem, then it's likely that they will continue shifting and shifting a lot.

And eventually it's going to actually make sense for them to do it.

—Russell Carleton is a former author of Baseball Prospectus and now an analyst for the New York Mets.

The State of the Quality Start

Rob Mains

One of the seven things you (probably) didn't know about the 2018 season is that quality starts—defined as a start lasting six or more innings with three or fewer earned runs allowed—as a percentage of total starts cratered to an all-time low of 41 percent. I want to look a little more deeply into this, since it's been a while (May of 2016, to be exact) since I've examined quality starts.

The term *quality start* is credited to *Philadelphia Inquirer* sportswriter John Lowe. It's been derided ever since he coined it in December of 1985. Three runs in six innings? That's a 4.50 ERA! In what world is that a measure of quality?

Let's start with that criticism. It's true that 3 x 9 / 6 = 4.5. (You came here for this sort of high-level math, right?) But it's also true that type of start, meeting the bare minimum for earning a quality start, is unusual. Here's the proportion of quality starts in which the pitcher lasted exactly six innings and yielded exactly three earned runs. (I'm going to confine this analysis to the 30-team era, 1998-present. Almost all data retrieved in this article is via the Baseball-Reference Play Index.)

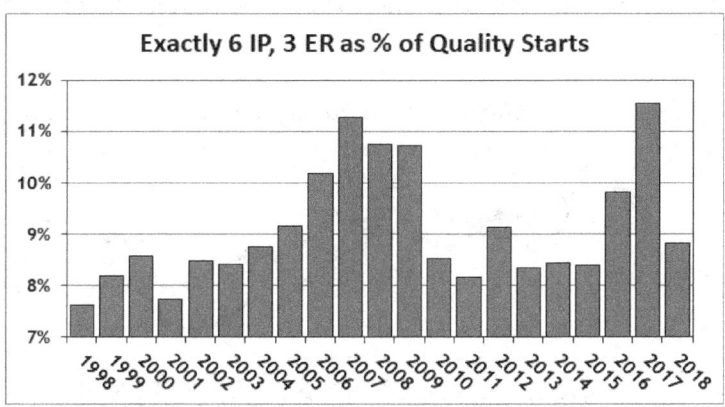

There were 1,997 quality starts in 2018. Only 176, or fewer than one in 11, featured a pitcher going six innings and allowing three earned runs. Put another way, the percentage of quality starts that resulted in a 4.50 ERA (8.8 percent) is less than half the percentage of games in which a batter hit two home runs and his team lost (22.5 percent; 237-69 won-lost). That doesn't impugn hitting two homers.

So if a 4.50 ERA isn't the norm, what is? How good are quality starts?

Pretty good, it turns out. First, on a team level:

Teams receiving a quality start from their pitcher won 68.4 percent of their games in 2018, in line with the 30-team era average of 67.9 percent. A team with a .684 winning percentage wins 111 games. Getting a quality start is definitely a good thing. Individual pitchers throwing quality starts have a higher winning percentage because a big slice of team losses is assigned to a reliever.

If teams do well in quality starts, how well do the starting pitchers do? Again, very well.

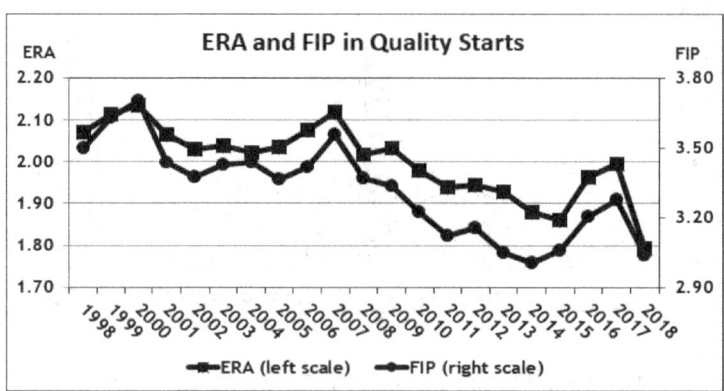

Pitchers in quality starts had a 1.79 ERA (blue line) in 2018, *the lowest in the 30-team era*. Their FIP was higher, 3.04, but still excellent. In the 30-team era, only 2014 had a lower FIP for quality starts, 3.01.

But, of course, the run environment in 2014 was different. Teams in 2014 scored 4.07 runs per game, the fewest in a non-strike year since 1976. They scored 4.45 runs per game in 2018. So surrendering a 3.04 FIP in 2018 is more impressive than 3.01 in 2014. Accordingly, let's look at ERA and FIP in quality starts relative to league averages.

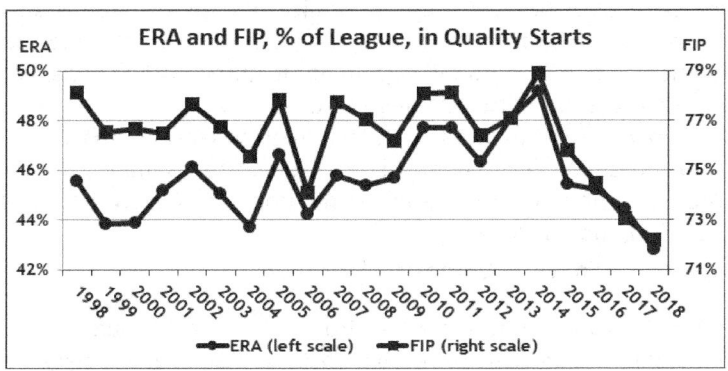

This tells a more dramatic story. Starting pitchers in 2018 gave up a 4.19 ERA and a 4.21 FIP. Starters in quality starts gave up a 1.79 ERA, 43 percent of the league average. Starters in quality starts gave up a 3.04 FIP, 72 percent of the league average. Both of these marks represent lows in the 30-team era.

The takeaway here is this: *Quality starts are better, relative to other starts, than they've ever been over the past 21 years.*

Maybe during the winter I'll look at this over a longer arc of time. For now, though, we can definitively say quality starts are the best they've ever been since the Diamondbacks and Rays joined the majors.

Yet, paradoxically, they're down.

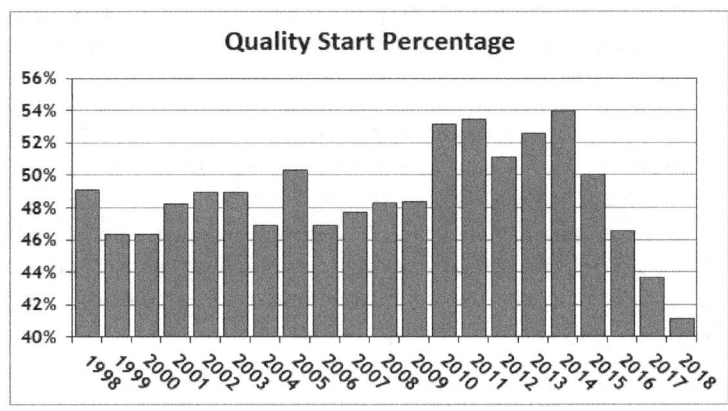

This graph covers only the 30-team era. In my article last week, though, I looked at the years 1908-2018. The result was the same. The 41 percent of starts in 2018 that were quality starts are an all-time low, well below the runners-up: 1930's 43 percent (the year teams scored an all-time record 5.55 runs per game) and last year's 44 percent.

The normal explanation for a dip in quality start percentage is an increase in scoring. When teams score a lot of runs, it's harder for starting pitchers to last six or more innings and limit opponents to three earned runs. From 1998 to 2014, the correlation between runs scored per game and the percentage of starts that were quality starts was -0.94. That means there was an extremely close relationship: More runs, fewer quality starts. Too small a sample? Go back to the start of the Expansion Era, 1961, and the relationship is even more negative, a -0.95 correlation, though 2014.

But that's broken down over the past four years:

- 2015: Runs per game increased from 4.07 to 4.25, quality start percentage decreased from 54.0 to 50.1. Yes, that's a negative relationship, but the regression model would predict a decline of 1.5 percentage points. We got 3.9 instead.
- 2016: Runs per game increased from 4.25 to 4.48, quality start percentage decreased from 50.1 to 46.6. Past experience would suggest a decline of just 1.8 percentage points. We got 3.4.
- 2017: Runs per game increased from 4.48 to 4.65, quality start percentage decreased from 46.6 to 43.6. Again, the direction's right, but the magnitude isn't. Using the relationship from 1998 to 2014, that increase in scoring should've reduced quality starts by 1.3 percentage points, not 2.9.
- 2018: Runs per game declined from 4.65 to 4.45. That should've resulted in the quality start percentage moving in the other direction, rising 1.6 points. It didn't. It fell 2.6 points, as noted, to an all-time low.

Granted, we're talking about just four years here. Maybe they're outliers. But I don't think they are. Quality starts, as noted, are as good or better than ever. But they're rarer than ever as well. And I think I know why.

To get a quality start, you need to allow three or fewer earned and pitch at least six innings. That's 18 outs. Here's a graph showing the number of starting pitchers who limited their opponents to three or fewer earned runs but got pulled after pitching at least five innings but fewer than six:

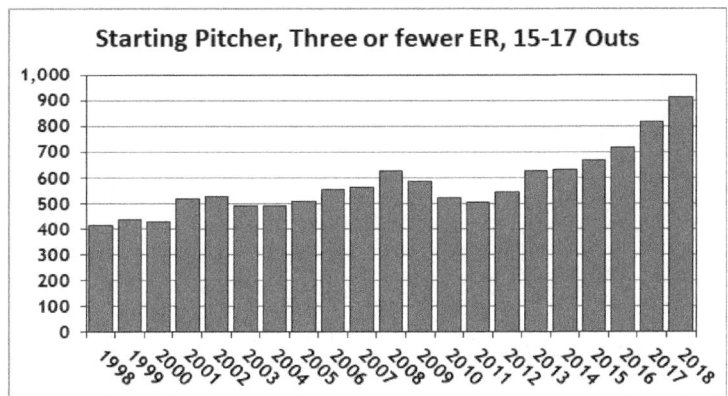

A pitcher getting 15 outs pitched five innings. A pitcher getting 16 outs pitched 5 1/3. A pitcher getting 17 outs pitched 5 2/3. More than ever before, pitchers are being removed from games in which they are within 1-3 outs of a quality start, falling just short of the six-inning finish line. Widespread acknowledgement of the times-through-the-order penalty and a flotilla of available bullpen arms is making the quality start simultaneously both more excellent and more rare.

Which is ironic, given that we saw a new post-war quality start record this season:

Rank	Pitcher	Season	Consecutive QS
1	Jacob deGrom	2018	24
2	Bob Gibson	1968	22
-	Chris Carpenter	2005	22
4	Johan Santana	2004	21
5	Luis Tiant	1968	20
-	Mike Scott	1986	20
-	Jake Arrieta	2015	20
8	Robin Roberts	1952	19
-	Tom Seaver	1973	19
-	Jack Morris	1983	19
-	Greg Maddux	1998	19
-	Josh Johnson	2010	19
-	Jon Lester	2014	19

While there have been longer streaks spread over multiple seasons, no pitcher since World War II threw more consecutive quality starts in one year than Jacob deGrom this year. The fact that he did in a year in which quality starts were the rarest they've ever been adds to the accomplishment.

—*Rob Mains is an author of Baseball Prospectus.*

Heads-Up Hacking—The First Pitch

Matthew Trueblood

Batters fell behind in a higher percentage of all plate appearances in 2018 than in any previous season for which we have pitch-by-pitch data. That kind of granular information goes back only to 1988, but we might safely assume (given all we know about baseball as it had been before that, and as it has been in the years since) that batters have *never* fallen behind at a higher rate than they did last season.

Through the 1990s, the percentage of all plate appearances that began 0-1 hovered in the high 30s and low 40s. In the 2000s, it rose steadily but slowly, through the mid-40s. In 2018, 49.8 percent of all trips to the plate began 0-1. That, as much as anything, captures in microcosm the nature of hitting in MLB today.

A countdown clock toward strike three begins ticking almost the moment a batter takes his place in the box. The league's adjusted OPS+ on the first pitch was higher in 2018 than ever before, and that has been true in most of the last 10 seasons. Batters hit .264/.289/.442 in all plate appearances in which they swung at the first pitch last season, and .241/.330/.395 in all plate appearances in which they took that first offering.

The percentage differences in batting average and isolated power there favor swinging at the first pitch by more than in any season since 1988, while the difference in on-base percentage favors taking by more than ever. If you want to get on base at a decent clip, it's a good idea to be patient, but you run the risk of missing the only chances you'll get to produce power.

Tampa Bay Rays 2019

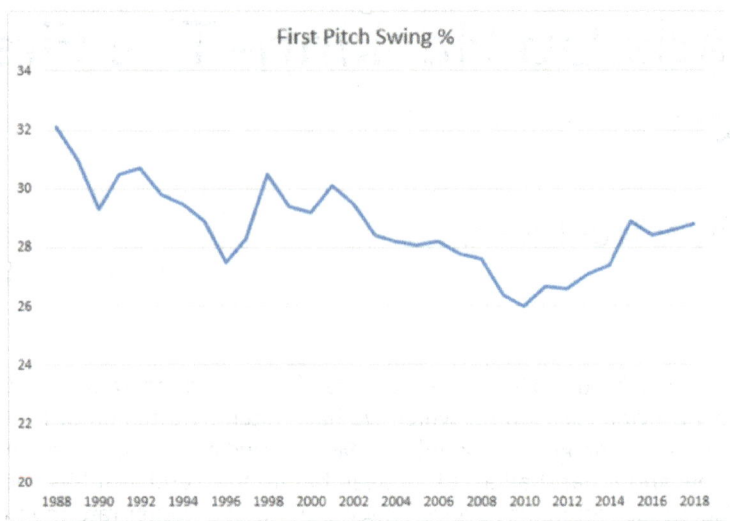

The league swung at the first pitch 28.8 percent of the time in 2018. With the isolated exception of 2015, that's the highest that number has climbed since 2002, but it might not be high enough. With the help of BP research maven Rob McQuown, I looked at the aggregate Called Strike Probability (CSProb) on the first pitch for each season since 2008, when the implementation of PITCHf/x first made measuring that possible. It's risen sharply during that period.

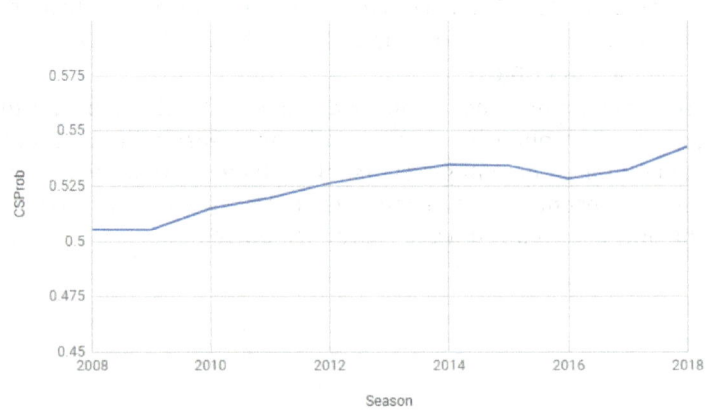

Called Strike Probability, First Pitch of PA (2008-2018)

Called Strike Probability is exactly what it sounds like: a pitch with a given CSProb has roughly that chance of being called a strike, if not swung at. In 2018, a batter who took 100 first pitches from a random sampling of the league's pitchers might expect to fall behind 54 or 55 times—up from 50 or 51 times in 2008. Almost regardless of pitch type (and, notably, especially in the case of fastballs), the first pitch tends to have more of the zone right now than ever before.

Pitchers are better at throwing strikes. They have better stuff, and believe more in their ability to miss bats within the zone. Perhaps most importantly, they know that batters are looking for one thing on the first pitch: a fastball. If they don't get it, they're likely to take the pitch. Check out how the use of sinkers and four-seamers on the first pitch has changed in a decade:

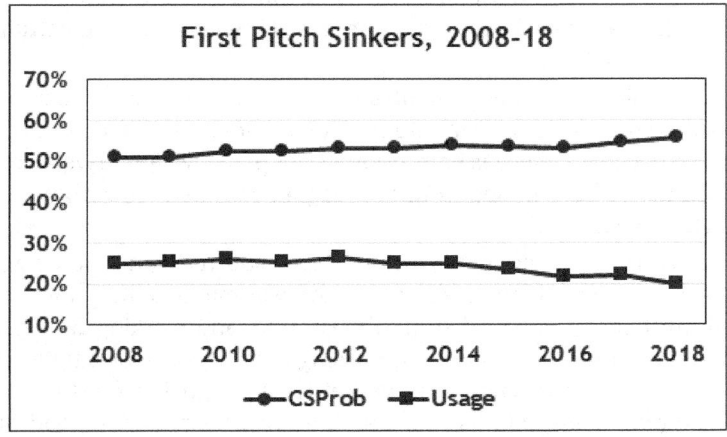

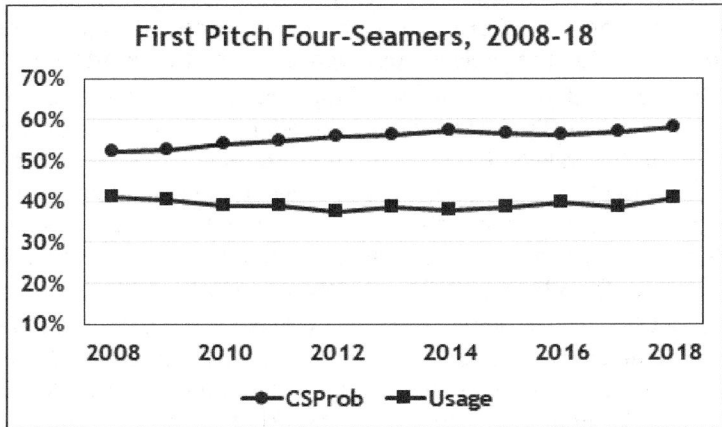

Tampa Bay Rays 2019

The sinker is losing its place in baseball, but the rate at which pitchers have thrown it on the first pitch hasn't dropped any faster than its usage rate in other counts. Pitchers have actually gone to their four-seamer *more* often to open counts, in the last few years, after a dip in the 2012-2015 period. What's really changed, though, and what shows up in both charts above, is that pitchers are catching more of the zone with first-pitch fastballs than they were a decade ago, or a half-decade ago. They're attacking right away, even with the pitch they know batters are expecting. The message is pretty clear: batters are being too passive.

Sliders, curves, and changeups each have more of the zone when thrown on the first pitch than they did several years ago, too, though the effect is less pronounced. Pitchers have seen the numbers; they know batters are doing better on the first pitch itself. They still feel safe throwing more and better strikes than ever before, figuring they'll come out ahead as long as they keep getting ahead to open each battle.

The Moneyball revolution brought an increased league-wide focus on OBP, which resulted in a de facto mandate to take a more patient tack at the plate. It worked very well for a while, as batters with poor plate discipline were compelled to either adjust or be expelled from the league, and pitchers with poor control were slowly weeded out.

However, concurrent with that revolution, and spurred by it in some ways, was the evolution of the pitching paradigm that now dominates the game. As batters ratcheted up their focus on inflating pitch counts and working walks, pitchers honed theirs on throwing strikes and missing bats. The league's understanding of what makes a good pitcher improved at least as much, from the mid-1990s through the mid-2000s, as its understanding of what makes a good hitter. As amphetamines and other performance-enhancing drugs were phased mostly out of the game, and as PITCHf/x broke onto the scene, individuals and teams learned how to exploit the evolved approaches of even the smartest hitters.

The ability to avoid making outs is still the most valuable one in baseball, but the magnitude of its eclipse of slugging is smaller than ever. To a greater extent than power, on-base skills derive their value from chaining—from the on-base skill levels of the players on either side of a given individual. Eleven years ago, when the housing crisis hit, people learned the hard way that the value of their homes depended a good deal on the values of their neighbors' homes. The same wasn't true, though, of their cars. So it is now, with OBP and SLG.

The global OBP in 2018 was .318. The only seasons since the Dead Ball Era in which the league got on base at a worse clip were 2013-2015, 1988, 1971-1972, and 1963-1968. This is all happening despite the aforementioned evolution of the science of hitting. It's happening despite a shift in approach and focus, one that would steer OBP ever higher, if only it were working.

Instead, it's sitting at a low ebb, and while it does so, even guys who get on base often are a little less helpful than they were 10 years ago—or 20, or 40, or 60, or 70, or 80, or 90. They're less helpful, that is, because unless there happen to be three or four other guys in the lineup who get on just as regularly, their contribution is merely to forestall the inevitable. Runs happen, increasingly, when a sudden bang happens, and that means attacking early in the count—because pitchers are sure as hell doing that.

In a league making contact on barely 75 percent of its swings, and a league in which an increasing number of pitchers can throw multiple off-speed pitches for strikes in any count, the only way to consistently generate offense is going to be aggressive. This isn't necessarily true for individuals, like Mookie Betts and Jose Ramirez, who make a lot of contact and have excellent plate discipline, and whose power comes from such natural quickness in a short stroke. Most players have to make tradeoffs, though, whether it be lowering their contact rate or raising their chase rate, in order to consistently make the quality of contact necessary to survive in today's game.

Highest %	Lowest %
Javier Baez – 48.3	Joe Mauer – 4.6
Freddie Freeman – 47.1	Mookie Betts – 9.7
Ozzie Albies – 46.3	Brett Gardner – 10.7
Jose Altuve – 44.2	Jose Ramirez – 12.0
Nick Castellanos – 44.1	Jason Kipnis – 13.8
Joey Gallo – 42.3	Jesus Aguilar – 14.5
Corey Dickerson – 40.9	Xander Bogaerts – 15.8
Salvador Perez – 40.8	Brian Dozier – 16.3
Eddie Rosario – 40.7	Mike Trout – 17.6
Nick Ahmed – 40.4	Yasmani Grandal – 17.6

Top 10 and Bottom 10 Hitters, First-Pitch Swing Rate (2018)

The question isn't which of these lists one prefers, but what they each convey, qualitatively, about the cat-and-mouse game of early-count hitting. Those top five on the left, especially, drive home the fact that for most players, getting aggressive early in the count is now key to keeping strikeout rate down and hitting for power.

For now, the message is: pitchers are coming right after batters with the nastiest stuff they've ever had. Batters had better stop giving away strike one and force hurlers to adjust, or the global OBP crisis is only going to get worse.

—*Matthew Trueblood is an author of Baseball Prospectus.*

A Hymn for the Index Stat

Patrick Dubuque

We survived without computers. I know this, because I remember the day when my dad hooked up his brand-new Atari 400 computer to the back of our 12-inch Magnavox television, and the perfect blue of the memo pad lit up for the first time. I was born just on the edge of that transitional generation, of learning cursive and balancing checkbooks and just doing math all the time, constant manual arithmetic.

It still amazes me. We learned how to sail ships without computers. We learned how to do calculus. We built towers that didn't fall down, most of the time. We engineered catapults to knock them down anyway. We built a robust system of philosophy called "utilitarianism," founded on the principle that the good of an action is evaluated by summing the effects of that action, which is the kind of formula that would make the world's mainframes crash. The whole foundation of statistics as a field is "here's math you could easily do but would die of old age first."

The fact of the matter is that there is too much math in the world to do. There are too many things changing, and too many things too small to notice, for us to handle. At some point, they become too much for the computers to handle as well, which is why we have chaos theory and undetectable earthquakes, but it's not an even fight. At some point, we fall back on intuition, and given how under-equipped we are, we're forced to bestow that intuition with some sort of supernatural superiority, the "gut feeling," that we can't prove because we can only intuit that our intuition is better.

We're all lousy at intuition, and wonderful at lying to ourselves about it. The honest truth is that computers are far better at intuition than we are, because in order to know what feels "off" you have to know what's "on." In order to do that you have to constantly reassess the average of everything, then re-rank your own experience against it.

Test your own, by comparing these three anonymous lines:

Player	G	HR	AVG	OBP	SLG
Player A	156	38	.259	.342	.535
Player B	154	38	.280	.348	.527
Player C	158	38	.266	.343	.509

These all seem like pretty similar players, right? The second one a touch more batted-ball dependent, the third a little less strong, but all pretty good hitters. And you'd be right, about the latter. Not the former.

Here's the breakdown:

- Player A: 1991 Howard Johnson, 141 DRC+
- Player B: 1996 Dean Palmer, 121 DRC+
- Player C: 2018 Giancarlo Stanton, 114 DRC+

Baseball is fortunate to have escaped the seismic shifts of so many other sports, where the talents and performances of other eras are nearly unrecognizable. (And not just other sports: try to explain the greatness of the movie Duck Soup without adjusting for era.) But they're still there, and they're nearly impossible to account for manually, without having to resort to sweeping generalizations like "steroid era" or juiced-ball era" to throw out entire swathes of production.

This is all to say that we should celebrate the index stat, that simple 100-based scale with such a humble aim: just to give context. It's hard to imagine how we lived without them for so long. Sabermetricians have always tried to make their stats look like other stats: True Average mapped to batting average, FIP molded to look like and compare to ERA. It's easy to understand the motivation—these statistics carry an emotional value in them that is hard to resist, as with the .300 hitter and the 2.00 ERA—but even they fall prey to the same loss of scale as their unadjusted counterparts. If a .300 average means different things in different years, does that hold true for a .300 True Average?

Instead, 100 doesn't say anything, except above average or below. And it does it instantly, for every season in every run environment for any statistic we want it to. We should have more index stats: K%+, so we can stop comparing Mike Clevinger's career 9.46 K/9 to Nolan Ryan's 9.55. HBP%+, so we can note that Ron Hunt was getting plunked when nobody else was getting plunked, as opposed to that imitator Brandon Guyer. Some might note how stale these references are and accuse league-adjustment as a backward-looking drive, and this is true. But we're always looking backward, always comparing the new with the expectations already set. The index stat just forces us to be honest.

There's always resistance to a new statistic, especially one so outwardly simple and so internally complex. We tend to stick with what we know, even in the case of formulas that are supposed to tell us what we know. But if your resistance is that it seems too complicated, too counterintuitive, too "black boxy," I encourage you to consider why you feel that way. Because the real world is infinitely more complicated than baseball, where all the pitches go in one basic direction and the baserunners are only allowed to travel in four directions. Baseball statistics based on mixed methodology are almost impossibly intricate. So are skyscrapers and automobiles. That's why we have computers—to take the guesswork out of them.

—*Patrick Dubuque is an author of Baseball Prospectus.*

Index of Names

Adames, Willy 22	Honeywell, Brent 91, 100
Alvarado, Jose 52	Kiermaier, Kevin 36
Alvarez, Roberto 109	Kittredge, Andrew 97
Arroyo, Christian 24	Kolarek, Adam 97
Banda, Anthony 97	Lacy, Rollie 97
Baz, Shane 89, 103	Liberatore, Matthew 92, 104
Beeks, Jalen 54	Linares, Resly 97, 108
Boldt, Ryan 96, 107	Lowe, Brandon 38, 105
Brujan, Vidal 79, 103	Lowe, Joshua 83
Castillo, Diego 56	Lowe, Nathaniel 84, 106
Chester, Carl 107	McCarthy, Joe 96
Chirinos, Yonny 58	McClanahan, Shane 93, 106
Choi, Ji-Man 26	McKay, Brendan 85, 94, 101
Ciuffo, Nick 80	Meadows, Austin 40
Cloyd, Tyler 97	Mercado, Michael 97
Diaz, Yandy 28	Merritt, Ryan 97
Dodson, Tanner 97, 108	Milner, Hoby 97
Dodson, Tanner 96	Moore, Andrew 97
Drake, Oliver 60	Morton, Charlie 67
Duffy, Matt 30	Mujica, Jose 108
Faria, Jacob 63	Myers, Tobias 97
Font, Wilmer 97	Pagan, Emilio 69
Fox, Lucius 96, 102	Perez, Michael 42
Franco, Wander 81, 99	Pham, Tommy 44
Frank, Tyler 96	Poche, Colin 95
Franklin, Austin 108	Pruitt, Austin 97
Garcia, Avisail 32	Robertson, Daniel 46
Gibaut, Ian 90	Rodriguez, David 96
Glasnow, Tyler 65	Roe, Chaz 97
Heredia, Guillermo 34	Romero, Tommy 109
Hernandez, Ronaldo 82, 105	Sadler, Casey 97

Sanchez, Jesus 86, 100
Santos, Luis 97
Schnell, Nick 96
Smolinski, Jake 96
Snell, Blake 71
Solak, Nick 87
Stanek, Ryne 73
Velazquez, Andrew 88
Wendle, Joey 48
Wong, Kean 96
Wood, Hunter 75
Yarbrough, Ryan 77
Zunino, Mike 50

Ballpark diagrams for Baseball Prospectus are created by THIRTY81Project, a design concept offering original ballpark artwork, including the new 'Ballparks of 2019' 11 x 17 color print.

Visit **www.thirty81project.com** for full details.

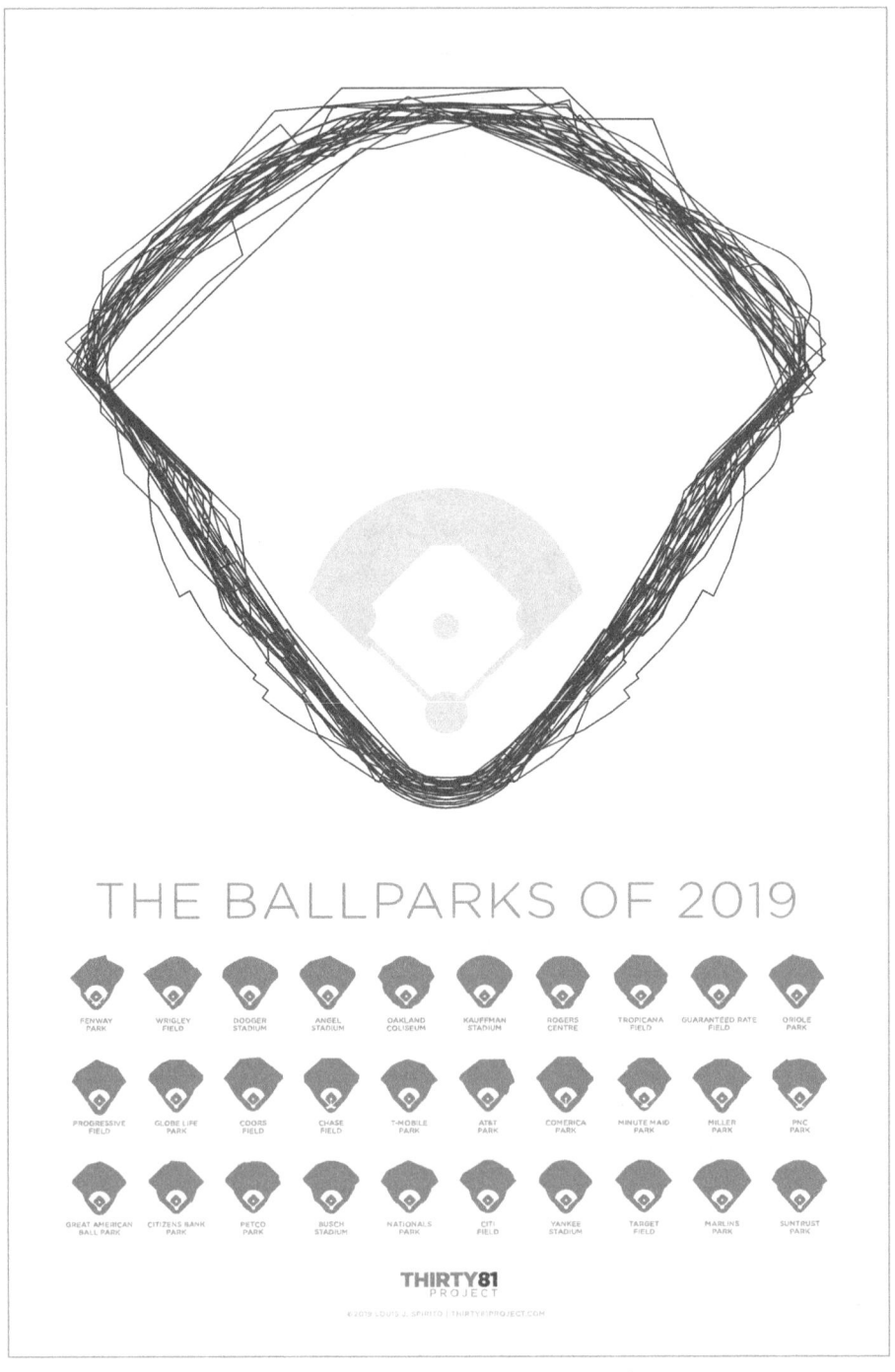